HOW TO STUDY

Fourth Edition

Ralph C. Preston

University of Pennsylvania

Morton Botel

University of Pennsylvania

SCIENCE RESEARCH ASSOCIATES, INC.
Chicago, Palo Alto, Toronto
Henley-on-Thames, Sydney
A Subsidiary of IBM

Library of Congress Cataloging in Publication Data

Preston, Ralph Clausius, 1908–
How to study.

1. Study, Method of.   I. Botel, Morton, joint author.   II. Title
LB1049.P7 1981   371.3   80-25547
ISBN 0-574-19625-0

10 9 8 7 6 5 4 3

Contents

Introduction   1

1   How to Plan Your Study Time and Setting   11

2   How to Master a Textbook Chapter: Previewing   25

3   How to Master a Textbook Chapter: Reading   35

4   How to Master a Textbook Chapter: Notetaking   49

5   How to Master a Textbook Chapter: Remembering   57

6   How to Listen More Effectively   69

7   How to Prepare for Examinations   87

8   How to Take Examinations   99

9   How to Broaden Your Reading Base   115

10 How to Write a Report   123

Conclusion: Reevaluating Your Study Habits   149

Practice Materials   155

Introduction

A skilled mechanic makes the repair of your automobile look simple. Watch skilled craft workers—a team of electricians wiring a house, for example. They work easily and quickly, and seem to enjoy their work. This is true of any good worker at his or her job.

Right now your work is studying, and your main job is being a student. As with every job, there are efficient and inefficient ways of getting the work done. Watch good students at work and you will discover that they proceed easily and quickly. They know what has to be done, and they they know how to do it with the least possible strain.

This book is about the skills you need in order to be an efficient student. There is nothing difficult about mastering these skills. Once you have acquired them, even the hardest courses will be easier for you. You will know what to do, how to do it, and you will get it done in far less time.

Psychologists have been working for a long time to find out how people learn and how they learn most easily. They have discovered shortcuts in studying and ways in which you can fix what you learn firmly in your memory. The psychologists have uncovered so much about learning—and what they have found is so easily utilized—that there is little excuse today for anyone to find studying hard, awkward, or excessively time-consuming.

STUDY SKILLS AND STUDY HABITS

Habits and skills are not the same. A study skill is a technique or method used to learn. Methods for spotting main ideas in reading and for memorizing a foreign-language vocabulary are study skills.

A study habit is a routine that you follow regularly. Keeping up to date in reading assignments, studying at the same time and place every day, and studying by yourself are study habits.

This book will outline the study skills that are essential to success and will help you master them. It will suggest study habits that will make your work easier.

HOW STUDY SKILLS AND HABITS HELP

You will gain more from this book if you know what you are looking for. What you should seek is some special gain, some special advantage to you from the procedures that are suggested.

Here are some possible advantages that may come from learning to study more efficiently:

1. You may improve the quality of your work. If you learn to study without difficulty, you will put your study time to better use. You will remember what you learn more easily, and you will remember it longer. As a result, you will have increased confidence in the classroom. Your contribution to class discussion and your writing will improve.

   Will you get better grades? That depends upon many factors, some of which you cannot control. But better study skills and study habits usually result in better work in recitations and on examinations. Usually, the payoff is higher grades.

2. You will probably enjoy your work more. No one enjoys doing something that he cannot do well. Dancing, swimming, reading, or playing tennis are little fun for the unskilled. If you read this book thoughtfully and apply its suggestions to your daily work, you will improve as a student. As you gain efficiency in studying, you will find pleasure in mastering even your most difficult assignments. You will also develop a new and surprising interest in your courses.

3. You should have more leisure time. If you build good study skills and habits, you will become a more efficient student. You will finish your studies in less time. This means you will have more time for leisure activities – social affairs, sports, hobbies, and just plain loafing.

4. You will have less to worry about. The average person is anxious about some things. But as you become a more efficient student and a better master of your studies, you will get rid of most worries about them – worries about exams, reports, and recitations.

IS THERE JUST ONE CORRECT WAY?

Are you bothered by the mention of skills and habits of study? Do you think you should be left to study in your own way? To be sure, there are individual styles of studying, just as there are individual styles of swimming, writing letters, and almost everything else. This book encourages you to develop your own style. Research shows, however, that successful students agree about the importance of certain basic skills and habits. It is these with which this book deals.

HOW IMPORTANT IS INTELLIGENCE?

Grades depend a good deal upon intelligence, but some of the most intelligent students get poor or mediocre marks. Students with less intelligence, by working efficiently and up to their capacity, receive excellent grades. After all, your teachers are grading not your intelligence but the quality of the work you do. It is important to make the most of your intelligence to get the best results possible. Good study habits and well-developed study skills will help you to do this.

Some students have achieved startling improvement in their studies after changing their study habits. The authors, who are themselves teachers, have heard enthusiastic comments from students who received their first A after using the mastery technique outlined in this book.

But getting high grades is only one of the many rewards of a good student. Even more important is the satisfaction that comes from a job well done – the best job you are capable of doing.

In addition, the study skills you learn in this book will make you more efficient as a person outside class. You will listen more attentively. You will have more to contribute to your friends, thus being a more interesting companion. You will get your work done faster with better performance.

CHECKING YOUR STUDY HABITS

On the next four pages you will find a study habits checklist. The checklist includes habits top college students believe to be most important.

Read each question in the checklist. Then answer it by marking an X in the appropriate box.

	Almost Always	*More than Half of the Time*	*About Half of the Time*	*Less than Half of the Time*	*Almost Never*
Planning Time					
*1. Do you keep up to date in your assignments?		X			
2. Do you have a study-schedule plan in which you set aside time each day for studying?					X

	Almost Always	More than Half of the Time	About Half of the Time	Less than Half of the Time	Almost Never
3. Do you divide your study time among the various subjects to be studied?				✗	
Arranging Physical Setting					
4. Is the space on your study desk or table large enough?	✗				
5. Is your study desk or table kept neat, that is, free of distracting objects?					✗
*6. Do you study in a quiet place — one that is free from noisy disturbances?				✗	
7. Do you study by yourself rather than with others?	✗				
8. When you sit down to study, do you have the equipment and materials you need?	✗				
Previewing					
9. Do you read over the table of contents of a book before you begin studying the book?					✗
10. Before studying an assignment in detail, do you make use of any of the clues in the book such as headings, illustrations, and chapter summaries?		✗			

	Almost Always	More than Half of the Time	About Half of the Time	Less than Half of the Time	Almost Never
Reading					
11. Do you try to get the meaning of important new words?					
12. As you read an assignment, do you have in mind questions that you are actually trying to answer?					
*13. Do you look for the main ideas in what you read?					
14. Are you able to read without saying each word to yourself?					
15. In addition to reading the required textbooks, do you read other materials for your courses?					
Notetaking While Reading					
16. As you read your assignments, do you take notes?					
17. Do you review your notes soon after taking them?					
Remembering					
18. Do you try to find a genuine interest in the subjects you study?					
*19. Do you try to understand thoroughly all material that you should remember?					

	Almost Always	More than Half of the Time	About Half of the Time	Less than Half of the Time	Almost Never
20. When studying material to be remembered, do you try to summarize it to yourself?			✓	✓	
21. Do you distribute the study of a lengthy assignment over several study sessions?		✓			
22. Do you try to relate what you are learning in one subject to what you learn in others?		✓			
Listening and Taking Class Notes					
23. During class, do you search for main ideas?					
*24. In class, do you take notes?		✓			
25. Do you revise class notes soon after class?				✓	
Preparing for Examinations					
*26. Before an examination, do you review the important facts and principles?				✓	
27. Do you combine important notes on your textbook and from class into a master outline in studying for a major examination?				✓	

	Almost Always	More than Half of the Time	About Half of the Time	Less than Half of the Time	Almost Never
28. Do you make up examination questions that you think will be asked, and answer them?					X
29. In studying for an examination, do you distribute your time over at least two sessions?					✓

Taking Examinations

*30. In taking examinations, do you read the directions and the questions with care?	✓				
31. At the start of an examination, do you make plans for suitably distributing your time among the questions?	✓				
32. In taking an essay examination, do you outline your answer to a question before you start answering it?	✓				
33. At the end of an examination, do you proof-read or check your answers?				✓	

Report Writing

| 34. Before writing a report, do you collect information by doing research in the library? | | ✓ | | | |

	Almost Always	More than Half of the Time	About Half of the Time	Less than Half of the Time	Almost Never
35. Before writing a report, do you make an outline?					
36. In writing a report, do you clearly indicate the main idea of each paragraph?					
37. In writing a report, do you rewrite your first drafts?					

Which questions did you answer "almost always" or "more than half of the time"? They represent your strong points as a student. Write down their numbers.

_____

_____

_____

Which ones did you mark "less than half the time" or "almost never"? Write down their numbers.

_____

_____

_____

These are your weak points.

Now look back at the questions represented by these numbers on the checklist to see which you believe to be your three greatest assets and which your three greatest weaknesses. Name them briefly.

Greatest assets:

1. _____

2. _____

3. _____

Greatest weaknesses:

1. _____

2. _____

3. _____

Now look at those questions in the checklist with an asterisk (1, 6, 13, 19, 24, 26, and 30). These questions are about practices that the best students in three colleges thought especially important. Which of these seven questions did you answer "almost always" or "about half" or "more than half of the time"?

_____

Continue these good practices. At the same time, while you are going through this book, give special attention to the suggestions dealing with the study habits in which you are weakest. Try to strengthen them.

1

How to Plan
Your Study Time
and Setting

If you are a typical student, you have a busy schedule. Your main goal is to complete your assignments on time and not let yourself fall behind. The secret is to plan your time.

At the outset this planning may be difficult. But after your first efforts, it will become easier and more natural with each succeeding semester. You will discover that by careful planning you can finish your daily work and still have leisure time.

If you have never planned your study time, you have probably had the uncomfortable experience of falling behind in one or more subjects. Because there is always new work to be done, it is hard to catch up. You struggle along, and just before exam time you try to make up back assignments and to cram by staying up nights. Exam week finds you exhausted, and you take your tests fatigued and nervous.

Probably everyone has experienced the unhappiness of this kind of poorly done job. But it can be avoided by a little time spent in planning a study schedule. Wouldn't it be satisfying to go to your exams knowing your term's work adequately, feeling refreshed, and being sufficiently wide-awake to communicate your knowledge accurately? Planning can help you do this.

Top students at three Pennsylvania colleges, polled on rules for success in study, considered keeping abreast of assignments one of the most important rules for good scholarship. If highly successful students consider it essential to keep up with assignments, the practice must certainly be recommended for every student.

SK 1: Make and keep a personal daily activity schedule.

The same plan for use of time will not suit every person, because people's activities vary widely in kind and time spent on them. There are those who need and want very detailed plans and rigid schedules. Others are more comfortable with only a minimum of planning and a very flexible schedule. The method of approach for most of us lies somewhere between these two extremes.

Have you ever tried making a breakdown on paper of your daily activities to see how much time you actually spend for classes, labs, assignments, and other required activities? If not, you may be surprised to find that they take less time than you expected and that you have more time for leisure than you imagined. Such a breakdown is the first step in working out a study schedule.

Following is a chart on which you can figure how you spend your time. Use the chart to indicate the number of hours per day and days per week you spend on each activity; multiply the two figures to find your weekly expenditure of time for each item. Add the last column to find the number of hours you spend on all your required activities during one week. Subtract this total from 168 (hours in one week), and divide your answers by 7 to give you your average daily number of free hours.

Activities Chart

Activities	*Hours per Day*	*Days per Week*	*Hours per Week*
Classes and labs			
Extracurricular activities			
Personal chores			
Job			
Study (Be realistic: put down double the number of weekly hours spent in classes for which you have regular assignments)			
Meals			
Sleep			

Activities	Hours per Day	Days per Week	Hours per Week
Other required activities			
Total			
Free time (subtract total from 168, number of hours in a week)			
Average free time for each day (divide above figure by 7)			

Two examples of plans are given on the next page, showing how two students with different planning ideas might schedule their time.

If you have already discovered an activity schedule that works well or if you have a plan in mind, write it in the chart on page 15.

If you do not have a plan, try to formulate one. Work it out on a separate sheet of paper and transfer the completed plan to page 15. Remember, this is a general plan. Free time must be allowed for special occasions such as an unexpected conference, a play rehearsal, or band practice.

After a while you may find weak spots in your plan. Perhaps you have budgeted too little sleep. Perhaps your history assignments usually require more time than you figured and your French a half hour less. Revise your schedule to fit your needs. Keep it flexible.

Make extra copies of your schedule and post them where you will see them frequently — on the wall of your room, on your dresser or desk, on your notebook cover. You've taken time to work out a practical plan. Now follow it!

TASK 2: Budget your study time.

When you start your first study period of the day, estimate how much time you will need for each subject or assignment that day. With that time budget in mind, start your first period of study.

Spend the first few minutes reviewing your last assignment in the subject. Include a rapid rereading of your most recent notes in that class to refresh your memory on the subject you will study. You will recall that this is part of the mastery technique.

This warm-up review will help you see the relation between material studied earlier and the new topic you will consider. For example, yester-

	Mon.	Tues.	Wed.	Thurs.	Fri.	Sat.	Sun.
7 – 7³⁰ am	Study						
7³⁰ – 8	Breakfast						
8 – 8⁴⁵	On way to campus					Breakfast	
8⁴⁵ – 9	Study					Study	
9 – 1 pm	Classes						Breakfast Church
1 – 2	Lunch					Free	Free
2 – 3³⁰	Classes						Study
3³⁰ – 5	Track and shower						
5 – 5³⁰	On way home						Free
5³⁰ – 6¹⁵	Free						
6¹⁵ – 7	Dinner						
7 – 8³⁰	Study						
8³⁰ – 9	Free						
9 – 10	Study						

	Mon.	Tues.	Wed.	Thurs.	Fri.	Sat.	Sun.
Before Breakfast	✕	✕	✕	✕	✕	Study	Study
Breakfast to lunch	Classes	Classes	Classes	Classes	Classes	✕	✕
Lunch to end of class	Classes	Classes	Classes	Classes	Classes	✕	✕
Between last class and dinner	✕	Study	✕	✕	✕	✕	✕
after dinner	Study	✕	Study	Study	Study	✕	Study

Your Personal Activity Plan

	Mon.	Tues.	Wed.	Thurs.	Fri.	Sat.	Sun.

day's discussion on Mendel's laws of heredity and today's lecture on mutations will align themselves in your mind. Without this review, you may overlook the framework into which your new topics fit.

Pick an assignment on which you worked yesterday, and note below some of the methods by which you can review it quickly.

1. _____

2. _____

3. _____

As you proceed with your studying, break up large blocks of study time. Suppose your general plan calls for three-hour sessions each weekday evening from seven to ten o'clock. For more efficient studying, break such long periods into spans of forty-five minutes to an hour each.

Take a short pause between periods. A break is especially desirable before you start studying a different subject. Ten minutes to play a favorite record, phone a friend, eat a light snack, or take a walk will be refreshing. The change will offset fatigue and allow you time to absorb, almost unconsciously, what you have been studying. Always keep the break short and relaxing.

On the following form plan your next large block of study time. How many minutes will you spend on each subject? How many minutes will you give yourself for a break? Decide what you will do at each break, and write it out.

	Subject	Number of Minutes	How Spent
Break			
Break			
Break			

The sincere desire to learn a lesson thoroughly or your special interest in a particular subject may lead you to devote so much time to it that there is too little time for other subjects. Such use of time could seriously affect your achievement in the neglected subjects.

You must therefore discipline yourself to follow your study-time budget. As you train yourself to follow your schedule, you will gradually find a pace that allows you to finish each subject in a given amount of time.

TASK 3: Keep physically active.

Too many students think of study as a passive process. The more passive you are, the more easily you will be distracted. The more actively you study, the better you will be able to concentrate. Take notes; underscore points and make marginal notes in the books you own; revise your lecture notes; diagram relationships in the subject matter; review completed sections by reciting to yourself. These are all aids to concentration. They will involve you actively in your studying. You will recall that detailed suggestions for carrying out these activities appear in chapters 1 through 4, which describe the mastery technique.

Select an assignment that you must work on tonight. Describe ways in which you can keep physically active during your study performance.

Subject _____

Specific assignment _____

Physical activities that would prove useful:

1. _____

2. _____

3. _____

TASK 4: Keep yourself free from disturbances.

This task may involve problems that each individual must solve in terms of the individual circumstances of his or her dormitory or home. The problems may stem from other people, the telephone, entertainment media, or other sources.

Some students like to study to the accompaniment of music. Research shows that radio or phonograph music will not necessarily cut down on reading or study efficiency; however, the effect varies from person to person. Test your own study efficiency with the radio or phonograph to determine whether it is distracting to you.

Make a list of disturbances that interrupt your study. Think of ways in which you can reduce them or eliminate them.

Disturbances That Interfere with Concentration	Ways to Reduce or Eliminate

TASK 5: Study by yourself most of the time.

Some of the most important study activities suggested in this book are best performed alone. An outline, for example, must be set up in *your* words. Your reading must be done at a speed consistent with *your* tempo, which depends upon *your* background and *your* familiarity with the subject matter. Bringing others in to work with you will only hamper your learning and waste your time. This does not mean that you will not benefit from discussing your subject matter with others between periods of study, or getting help from them when you need it. On the contrary, talking over your studies with someone else is stimulating and is a valuable means of recitation and review. Mastering a subject, however, requires that you work independently most of the time.

Studying with a friend or two may be beneficial, but not if you are dependent on it. That will delay your becoming a self-assured, independent student.

How often do you study with others? _____

_____

What are the advantages? _____

_____

_____

How could some of these advantages, if any, be supplied through individual study?

_____

_____

TASK 6. Locate and learn how to use a study desk.

Have a desk or table that you can call your own. Select one with a roomy surface so that you can spread out your work and not feel cramped. You will need plenty of space for assignments that require the use of several books and notebooks at the same time. Make sure the surface of the desk is smooth and hard, not pitted or grooved, so that you can write smoothly.

Keep the desk surface clear when it is not in use; then it is ready for your next study session. Never permit it to become a catchall. You should be able to sit down to study at any time and to lay out your books and other materials without having to clear away disorders. Your study desk is not a good permanent place for such things as calendars, photos, knickknacks, or clocks. Reserve this desk or table strictly for studying.

Your choice of a chair to fit the desk is also important. It should be comfortable but not too comfortable. It should be designed for sitting upright, not for lounging. Its height should be such that when you are seated the desk's surface will be a little higher than your waist.

Discipline yourself to start studying as soon as you sit down at your desk. Soon you will find that you do it automatically. Some students find it helpful before they start to list any thoughts or problems that could hinder their concentration. These might include a phone call that should be made or any personal problem. Consider, first, possible distractions, or decide when you can give them your complete attention. This will help clear your mind for serious study.

TASK 7: Have your desk well lighted.

Lighting makes a difference in the efficiency of your study. Poor lighting causes fatigue and eyestrain, both of which are enemies of concentration. Your desk should be so well lighted that you can work as well at night as during the day.

Artificial lighting can come from overhead, a floor lamp, or a desk lamp—as long as enough light reaches your desk. Authorities regard indirect lighting as superior to the direct lighting provided by spotlight lamps, which illuminate only part of your desk and create deep shadows or glare. An adequate lamp will illuminate your entire desk area evenly. Test the adequacy of your lighting by placing a book at different points on your desk to see if you can read the small print easily in each position. The rest of the room should also be well lit, without dark shadows.

Try not to face a window or the source of light. Place your desk so that the principal light comes from behind you or over your left shoulder (or right shoulder if you write with your left hand). Then you will not face the glare, and the light will not throw a shadow on what you are writing.

Describe your present lighting arrangement and tell how it could be improved.

_____

_____

_____

_____

_____

_____

_____

_____

_____

_____

_____

TASK 8: Have necessary study materials and tools conveniently at hand.

Study materials should be kept in the desk drawers or on nearby shelves.

Following are listed the materials that students should usually have within reach. You may find that some are more important than others, but you will probably use all of them at one time or another.

On the blank lines, add any items you need that are not listed. Then go through the entire list, placing a check in the correct column for each item.

Your Personal Study Materials and Tools

	Always Have on Hand	Some- times Needed	Not Needed
Reference Books Dictionary			
Atlas 1-vol. book of facts (like World Almanac)			
Paper Lined notebook paper			
Unlined notebook paper			
Lined composition paper ($8\frac{1}{2} \times 11$)			
Typing paper ($8\frac{1}{2} \times 11$)			
Tracing paper			
Graph paper			
Carbon paper			
Miscellaneous Typewriter			
Pencils			
Colored pencils			
Pen			
Ink eraser			
Ink eradicator			
Knife or pencil sharpener			

	Always Have on Hand	*Sometimes Needed*	*Not Needed*
Ruler			
Stapler and staples			
Compass			
Protractor			
Paper punch			
Ink or ballpoint refills			
Paste or glue			
Scotch tape			
Paper clips			
Gummed ring reinforcements			
Rubber bands			
Scissors			
Other			

A Bird's-Eye View of Your Time and Setting for Study

1. Make and keep activity schedule.
2. Budget study time.
3. Keep physically active.
4. Free yourself from disturbances.
5. Study by yourself.
6. Have a desk exclusively for study.
7. Have good lighting.
8. Have study materials at hand.

2

How to Master
a Textbook Chapter:
PREVIEWING

Probably the most common assignment you get as a student is to read and master a section or a chapter of some textbook. How can you do this most efficiently? How do you use the organization of your books to relate the whole to the parts and the parts to the whole? What kind of notes should you take? Will you remember what you have read? You will find the answers to such questions in a systematized method of study called the mastery technique.

The mastery technique is a method for helping you master your reading assignments. It consists of four parts:

      I.   Previewing
     II.   Reading
    III.   Notetaking
    IV.   Remembering

While these seem to be four separate activities, they actually overlap. Your goal is learning to combine them in a single operation. When you have gained this skill, you will save the hours that you now waste in rereading.

Speeding up your study is not the only advantage you will derive from the mastery technique. You will understand better what you are studying, and you will remember it longer. Furthermore, you will have greater interest in your studies.

You may already be aware that many texts are highly structured, or organized: that is, the books are divided into units, the units into chapters, the chapters into sections, and the sections into subsections. The authors and editors of your books use these divisions and other signaling devices such as tables of contents, introductory and concluding paragraphs, pictures and charts, and typographical devices such as italics and bold-face type, to indicate the main parts of their presentation and how they are related.

Few students give proper attention to this structure or outline. More important, they fail to use this signaling system to analyze the whole picture. As a result, they have difficulty concentrating when they start to study. They read very slowly or they have to reread to get their bearings.

To correct such time-wasting and inefficient ways of studying, you will want to get from the signaling system the entire structure of the book you are using. This is really the first step in reading a textbook or any reading assignment. It is called previewing. It tells you how the whole is related to the parts.

Previewing a reading assignment means studying the organization of the book or the assigned portion of a book. It means thumbing through its pages to get a general picture of the total subject before you do any systematic reading.

You will be more efficient if you take the trouble to preview. You will concentrate better, understand more readily, and see more clearly the relation between ideas in the assignment. Previewing saves time in the end.

TASK 1:   Before reading any of the chapters, examine the book as a whole.

Who is the author? Is his or her position as a professional person given? When was it published? Has it been revised since its original publication?

Why might the answers to these questions be important?

_____

_____

Another part of a book to preview is the table of contents. Let us suppose you have been assigned this chapter in this book. Before reading the chapter further, take a look at its table of contents. You will find that this chapter is one of four with the same main title. This should give you the basis for anticipating the high degree of relationship between the four chapters. The titles of succeeding chapters should provide clues that mastering a textbook is related to other reading, report writing, listening, taking examinations, and additional aspects of studying and learning.

Now preview an actual reading assignment that you have not yet started. Choose an assignment on which all the previewing tasks can be tried. Then fill in the following form.

Name of subject _____

Title of book in which reading has been assigned _____

_____

Author _____

Section of book assigned _____

_____

Copy below that part of the table of contents for the chapter in which the assignment appears.

_____

_____

Look over the table of contents. What other chapter or chapters in the book deal with the same phase of the subject matter?

_____

_____

_____

_____

_____

What phase or phases of the subject do these other chapters deal with?

_____

_____

_____

_____

Judging only from the table of contents, state in a sentence or two what you expect to learn from this reading assignment.

Roman Empire in depth. How they dealt with Christians, how consistently resisted her

In the same way, you can look over the table of contents of any book and find quickly the topics that will be covered and in what order. Knowing the general plan of a chapter in advance will give your reading a sense of direction. If the assignment covers only part of a chapter, you should still preview the entire chapter.

Now see if you have a textbook that has a glossary (that is, a list of the meanings of specialized terms of importance to the subject). Glossaries are usually placed near the back of a book and arranged alphabetically. If you have a book with a glossary, read the meanings given for two or three of the terms listed there.

In what ways will the glossary be useful to you? Give an example.

Many textbooks have indexes. Look through the index of one of your textbooks. How is it likely to be of use to you? Give an example.

TASK 2:   Look over the section headings and make a preliminary outline.

Most textbook chapters are organized into sections, each of which has a heading. For example, this chapter has the following headings:

TASK 1:   Before reading any of the chapters, examine the book as a whole (page 26).

TASK 2:   Look over the section headings and make a preliminary outline (page 28).

TASK 3:   Read the first and last paragraphs of the assigned chapter (page 31).

TASK 4:   Study the pictorial aids (page 32).

TASK 5:   Take an inventory. Ask yours lf, "What do I know about the chapter at this point?" (page 32).

Not only in previewing, but in each part of the mastery technique, one of the basic jobs is to spot and record important words and their meanings. Look particularly for key words in the headings. This is the beginning of your vocabulary study. For example, one heading in a text on government reads:

"Advantages of Bicameral Government"

If you have not had a course in government, you might not know the meaning of *bicameral*. This would be a word for you to spot and record.

Run through the headings of a textbook you are now using. Give an example of a heading with an unfamiliar word.

(handwritten response)

Here is an example of a preliminary outline of this chapter. Of course each student may have a somewhat different outline.

Master Textbook

Mastery Technique: Previewing

1. Table of Contents
2. Preliminary Outline
3. First and Last Paragraphs
4. Pictorial Aids
5. Inventory

Now, in the following space develop your own preliminary outline of a chapter in the textbook you selected to practice the previewing tasks.

Your Example of a Preliminary Outline of a Chapter

TASK 3:   Read the first and last paragraphs of the assigned chapter.

Another step in previewing an assignment is to read the first and last paragraphs of the assigned chapter before you begin to read the whole chapter. Most textbook chapters introduce the subject matter in an opening paragraph and summarize it in a final paragraph.

Sometimes the author uses two or three paragraphs to introduce and summarize the chapter. If you do not find ample information in the first or last paragraph, read the second and third paragraphs at each end of the chapter for your preview. If they also are unsatisfactory for preview purposes, then disregard this task for the chapter in question.

Read the first three paragraphs of this chapter. They tell you that the early chapters describe the mastery technique, a technique that can help you learn how to master a chapter. The next few paragraphs introduce the practice of previewing. They present previewing as the first step in mastering a chapter. They describe it as a method of learning the organization or structure of a book or of a chapter. You are told that previewing will increase your efficiency, concentration, and understanding.

Now turn to the last section of this chapter on page 33. You will see that the authors use a device called "A Bird's-Eye View of Previewing" to summarize. It indicates the five key steps of previewing in outline form.

Do this reading task for the assignment that you described on page 27. If the assignment consists of more than one chapter, try the task for the first of those chapters. Use the entire chapter even if the assignment consists of less than a chapter.

What the first paragraph or section tells

_____

_____

_____

What the last paragraph or section tells

_____

_____

_____

_____

TASK 4: Study the pictorial aids.

The next step in previewing is to look at any pictures, tables, maps, charts, and outlines in the book. The example of a preliminary outline in task 2 of this chapter is a graphic illustration.

Most textbooks have some pictorial aids in each chapter. They are put into the book to illustrate something the author thinks important. Study the aids you find in the pages of your reading assignment. You will be taking another important step in your preview.

Again refer to the assignment you described on page 27. List the titles of three pictorial aids you find in the assigned pages.

1. _____

2. _____

3. _____

What important idea of the chapter is clarified or explained by each of these aids?

1. _____

2. _____

3. _____

TASK 5: Take an inventory. Ask yourself, "What do I know about the chapter at this point?"

Try to remember what you learned by looking over the table of contents, scanning the section headings, reading the first and last paragraphs of each chapter, and studying the pictorial aids. In a preview of this chapter, your inventory might run something like this:

"This chapter describes a method for mastering textbook reading assignments. This method, called the mastery technique, is discussed in the first four chapters. It consists of four steps: previewing, reading, note-taking, remembering. The tasks in previewing include using the table of contents, making a preliminary outline, reading introductory and concluding paragraphs, using pictorial aids, and taking an inventory."

It is quite clear that you can learn a great deal about a chapter without actually reading it. Previewing an assignment may take five or ten minutes of your study hour, but this is not time wasted. Previewing will save you many times the minutes you spend on it, because it prepares you for better understanding and faster reading. A by-product of previewing is better remembering.

Take an inventory of your knowledge (ask yourself, "What do I know now?") of the assignment you have been previewing, which you described on page 27. Write it out in the space below. Practice in putting an inventory into precise words will assure you that you know what is involved. Usually you need not take the time to write out the inventory; you can just think it through.

EXTRA PRACTICE

Turn to the practice material on "City Planning" on page 154.
1. Read the headings and make a preliminary outline. (Save the outline for "Extra Practice" exercises following Chapters 4 and 5.)
2. Read the first and last paragraphs.
3. Tell someone what you now know about the selection before having actually read it.

Practice these three exercises on the material on "Latitude and Longitude" (page 156), "The Moon's Movements" (page 158), "Psychology" (page 159), and "Vitamins" (page 164).

A Bird's-Eye View of Previewing

1. Read over the table of contents.
2. Look over section headings and make a preliminary outline.
3. Read first and last paragraphs of chapter.
4. Study pictorial aids.
5. Take an inventory.

3

How to Master
a Textbook Chapter:
READING

Successful reading of an assignment requires active thinking. What you derive from your reading depends to some extent on what you bring to it by way of your background and your plan of attack.

Your background includes your interests, knowledge, intelligence, and curiosity.

Your plan of attack should include two main thrusts. The first is concerned with spotting, determining the meaning of, and keeping a record of key vocabulary. The second is concerned with using questions to guide your reading and with reading and reciting to yourself. The tasks in this chapter on reading, therefore, are divided into these major areas of emphasis: (1) vocabulary development and (2) reading with questions in mind. When the activities of the mastery technique have become part of your habit pattern, of course these two kinds of activities will merge into a unified study technique.

THE READING VOCABULARY TASKS

Research has shown that by adding to your vocabulary you can increase your success in school and speed your reading. Not knowing the meaning of words slows you down. When you come across a word you do not know, you probably do one of the following things: (1) You skip over it. (2) You continue and find it hard to concentrate because you do not understand completely. (3) You find the reading to be difficult and slow. You may then decide to reread, and this retards you even more. (4) You look up the word in the dictionary, or you ask someone its meaning; either is an intelligent thing to do but takes time.

Clearly, then, the more words you know well the less frequently you will have to slow down; the larger and more accurate your general vocabulary, the faster your grasp will be of most reading matter.

Give an example from a previous or current assignment when you were slowed down by not knowing the meaning of a word.

Subject _____

Textbook _____

Word _____

Sentence in which word appeared _____

_____

_____

How were you slowed down? Place a check after the correct answer.

You skipped over the word, and comprehension trouble followed.   _____

You stopped to look up the word in a dictionary.   _____

You stopped to ask someone the meaning of the word.   _____

Other (explain)   _____

_____

_____

Practicing the five vocabulary tasks that follow will greatly enhance your vocabulary, thus increasing your reading efficiency and your general success in school.

TASK 1:   Spot unfamiliar words as you read.

As a student, you constantly encounter unfamiliar or little-known words. Are you aware of this, or have you developed a habit of ignoring them? Skipping over unfamiliar words is not efficient studying and of course is no help in building a better vocabulary. Developing better word knowledge requires constant awareness and noting of unfamiliar words.

If the spotting of unfamiliar words is new to you, begin by detecting strange terms in your textbooks. This gives you a concrete basis on which to work. During your preview of a reading assignment you have noticed that authors of textbooks often call attention to important words by setting them in boldface type or italics or by underlining them. A sentence from one textbook reads: "The earth's oldest rocks are *igneous*."

Give an example of a sentence containing an unfamiliar word in bold-face or italic type from one of your textbooks. Underline the word.

_____

_____

TASK 2:   Learn to obtain word meanings from context.

You can't depend entirely on context—it could produce some pretty wild guessing that would often lead you *away* from the word's true meaning. Nevertheless, to improve your vocabulary you must develop a certain amount of independence, and you can do this by learning to figure out some words for yourself.

Look at this sentence: The darkness was impenetrable, so he lit a match. If you do not know the meaning of *impenetrable*, you may conclude from the rest of the sentence that "the darkness was very dark"! Such a conclusion is a reasonable one, even though it gives you only a vague meaning of the word *impenetrable*.

When you encounter an unfamiliar word, it often pays to read a bit farther to see if the author explains it. Note in the following passage how the word *ignominy* is clarified:

> There I stood before all my classmates, covered with ignominy. Never in my life have I been so embarrassed.

You might very well guess from the second sentence that *ignominy* means disgrace or humiliation.

Use the total meaning of the following passages to help you get the meaning of the underlined words. After completing this exercise, check your answers with a dictionary.

*The manager is **intransigent** concerning the amount of a beginner's salary. He will not budge.*

__Intransigent__ probably means ___stubborn_____

_____

*Unlike other hawks, the **accipiters** combine a small head, short wings, and a long tail.*

*An **accipiter** is a* _____

*No one regretted the passing of such a **meretricious** newspaper. Its headlines attracted the eye effectively enough, but its treatment of news was shamefully cheap and unworthy.*

Meretricious *probably means* _____

_____

TASK 3:   Use a dictionary to find word meanings.

When you spot an unfamiliar word not made clear by the context, look it up in the dictionary. A dictionary is one of your most important study tools.

Read the following sentence and think about its meaning:

Self-determination is a criterion of a nation's growth.

Express your understanding of the sentence in your own words without using a dictionary.

_____

_____

Now look up the words self-determination *and* criterion *in a dictionary and find a definition that comes closest to fitting each as used in the example sentence. Even if you think you already know the meaning of one or both of these words, look them up. You may discover that your ideas about them are unclear or inaccurate.*

Definitions that fit the example sentence:

self-determination _____

_____

criterion _____

_____

Rewrite your understanding of the sentence in the light of these dictionary definitions. You are unusual if you find your original definition adequate.

_____

_____

_____

Your second statement is likely to be sharper and more accurate than your first, because you now know the exact meaning of all the words. This will always be true: the more thorough your knowledge of words, the sharper will be your understanding of the ideas you read and hear.

When you use the dictionary, if several meanings are given for a word, how will you know which one is correct for your purpose? You will need to choose the definition that fits the sense of what you are reading.

For example, suppose you are looking up the meaning of a word like *script* in the sentence below:

Skilled stage direction is of little use if the script is dull.

Let us suppose the dictionary you are using gives five definitions of *script:*

1. A document
2. A system of writing
3. Type that is an imitation of writing
4. The book of a play or movie
5. Abbreviation of manuscript

The fourth meaning is the one that applies to "skilled stage direction."

Look up in the dictionary five unfamiliar words from the textbook you referred to on page 37. Locate the meanings of the words that fit the context of the sentences in which you found them, and copy the definitions below.

Page Number	Word	Definition

TASK 4:   Collect and record unfamiliar words.

It is not enough to spot and look up unfamiliar words. Collect them. Keep a notebook or a card file for recording them. If you choose the notebook method, prepare columns for each page as suggested on the next page. An example of the recording of one word is shown.

Add the five unfamiliar words you looked up in the dictionary for task 3. In the "Meaning as Used" column, write a short definition in your own words. This will help you grasp and remember the word meaning.

Word	Phrase or Sentence in Which Used	Meaning as Used	Other Important Meanings
paraphrased	The editor of this modernized Chaucer has paraphrased a great deal.	to restate in other words	no other meaning

If you prefer to keep a card file instead of a notebook, you will do well to buy several packs of 3 × 5 index cards and an oversize file box (6 to 8 inches long) in which to keep them. Put the same kind of information on the cards as was suggested for a notebook. The arrangement will have to be different, because there will not be room for all the columns. Each item will fit more conveniently on a separate horizontal line, as in this example:

Now give an example of your own.

TASK 5:   Use and review the new words.

Your next job is to become thoroughly acquainted with your recorded unfamiliar words through use and review. Try to use each new word in at least two different conversations even if it seems artificial or unnatural. You will feel more at home with a new word if you hear yourself say it.

Use the new words in writing, too, whenever you have a suitable opportunity. For example, if you have just learned *paraphrase* and are preparing a composition on capitalism, you could write:

One argument for keeping capitalism is that (to paraphrase Shakespeare) it is safer to get along with our present ills than to fly to others that we don't know about.

Make plans for using one of the new words that you have recorded in this chapter.

Word _____

A sentence in which it could be used in conversation _____

_____

A sentence in which you could write it _____

_____

New words should be reviewed until you feel well acquainted with them. Words that you can start using right away and fairly frequently (you will be surprised how many fit into this category) will not, of course, need any intensive reviewing. Think about the others and look at them frequently. A good practice is to go over the words in your notebook or card file once a week. See if you can use each word in a sentence before looking at the definition. Vary the procedure occasionally by having someone name the word for you to define and put into a sentence.

With practice like this, your word power will grow rapidly. As your list grows, you will be able to recognize instantly the meaning of words you have previously recorded and reviewed.

THE READING-WITH-QUESTIONS TASKS

Research has shown that if you read to find answers to questions rather than just to cover the pages assigned, you get much more from your reading. Practice the following tasks that involve posing questions and answering them while reading. When you reach the point where you do this automatically, you will greatly increase your efficiency as a reader.

TASK 1:   Pose questions to guide your reading.

If you read searchingly rather than just cover the pages assigned, you will understand the ideas and their relationships better. The best searching strategy is to make up your own questions and recite the answers until you are satisfied that you have grasped the key ideas. But there is a second strategy that you should also learn. It consists of looking for each main idea as you read and thinking of a question that the main idea answers.

Using the first strategy, you turn each heading into a question and, as you read, look for the answer until you come to the next heading. That is how you make use of the book's signalling system. Headings and headlines are used by authors to signal the major ideas and their relationships.

Using the second strategy, you read until you know you have covered a main point. (A main point is an idea that is developed in a paragraph or two; a main point is accompanied by two or more details or small points to support it.) Often a single sentence in a paragraph states that paragraph's main idea. After locating a main point, think of a question that is answered by it.

Refer to a reading assignment that you must complete within the next few days. List the first three headings from it in the left-hand column below. Then make up a question or questions suggested by each heading and list them in the right-hand column opposite the headings.

Name of textbook _____

Title of chapter _____

Pages assigned _____

Heading from Book	*Question or Questions It Suggests*
1.	
2.	
3.	

Using the same assignment, try the second strategy. Go on past the first three headed sections. Read to find the next three main ideas and write each as a question.

Main Idea	*Question or Questions It Answers*
4.	
5.	
6.	

Practice both approaches or combinations of them until you find a strategy that feels good to you.

TASK 2:   Check your understanding by reciting the answers.

After finding an answer to a question, repeat it to yourself. This is insurance against a merely vague feeling that you know the answer. Stop reading at the end of each section and tell yourself the answers to the questions in your own words. This is sometimes called reciting. Reciting in this way helps you to remember the ideas. It also serves as a check of how thoroughly you understand what you read.

Now, practice reciting by recording below your answers to questions you posed on the preceding page. Number your answers to match the questions.

Heading 1

_____

_____

_____

_____

_____

Heading 2

_____

_____

_____

_____

_____

Heading 3

_____

Main Idea 4

Main Idea 5

Main Idea 6

TASK 3: Reread when necessary to clarify any ideas of which you are unsure.

If you feel your understanding of a section is incomplete after you have read and recited it, read the heading once more and frame a new question in your mind. Then reread the passage until you are sure you can answer the question satisfactorily.

TASK 4: Reflect on your reading.

There is much more to reading than finding out what the author is saying directly. Good readers read critically. The critical reader is always thinking from several points of view while reading.

Readers who do not respond critically leave themselves out of the reading. They accept blindly that the printed word is total truth or that their own ideas about the text are unworthy. It is essential that we not only understand an author but also become truly involved with the many levels of meaning in everything we read.

These ways of thinking (or reflecting, or questioning) can be classified into three categories: (1) Responding to the ideas of the text at a personal level; (2) Reading between the lines; and (3) Making judgments about the value of the reading.

1. The Personal Response. Write a personal response to something you have read recently. Express how it made you feel or what, in your own life, it reminded you of. All such personal responses are part of the meanings everything contains. Notice in book reviews how much the reviewers bring in their own views.

Share your ideas with other students who have done the same reading you have done. See the many ways different readers see things from their own points of view.

———————————————————————————————————

———————————————————————————————————

———————————————————————————————————

———————————————————————————————————

2. Reading between the Lines. The critical reader is always thinking things like: "What can I do with these ideas? What is this author's authority for his statements? Is the author trying to persuade me to do something? Is the author really objective, as he says he is, or is he prejudiced? Is he angry? Is he cynical? What other interpretations are possible, given the same facts?"

3. Making Judgments. The critical reader answers some of these questions. He decides whether the writing is good or bad, how carefully researched it is, how moral the ideas are, and so forth.

Write a response to something you have recently read. Again, share your ideas with classmates. Describe below the wide range of their thinking.

_____

_____

_____

_____

EXTRA PRACTICE

Turn to the practice material on "City Planning" on page 155.

1. *Make a list of unfamiliar words as you read, and get their meanings in one of the ways suggested in this chapter.*
2. *Turn each heading as you come to it into a question and let that question guide your reading. Write down the questions.*
3. *After you finish reading the selection, recite the answers to yourself.*

Practice these three exercises on the material on "Latitude and Longitude" (page 157), "The Moon's Movements" (page 159), "Psychology" (page 161), and "Vitamins" (page 165).

A Bird's-Eye View of Reading

The Reading Vocabulary Tasks

1. Spot unfamiliar words as you read.
2. Get word meanings from context.
3. Use a dictionary.
4. Collect and record unfamiliar words.
5. Use and review new words.

The Reading-with-Questions Tasks

1. Pose questions as you read.
2. Recite answers to yourself.
3. Reread when uncertain.
4. Reflect on your reading.

How to Master
a Textbook Chapter:
NOTETAKING

Notetaking is one of the fine arts of study. Learn to practice it as an art. Most students who take notes on their reading spend too much time on them. They put down too many details. Some students actually give up notetaking because it seems much too time-consuming. But most good students take notes, and everyone should learn to do so efficiently.

Your notes should contain key words or phrases to summarize the important ideas you read. They should contain the words that will help you remember best the key facts and ideas.

What do you think are good reasons for taking notes?

_____

_____

_____

Compare your reasons with those given below.

1. Taking notes will keep you looking for main facts and ideas and will force you to try to separate the main points from less important points.

2. Taking notes will help keep your interest alive by varying your study activities. Reading all of a lengthy assignment at one sitting can be tedious.
3. Taking notes will give you a bird's-eye view of what the author is saying. Your notes should make it possible for you to recall the main ideas and their relationship, months or even years after you have taken them.
4. Taking notes makes for efficiency. It is a form of recitation. If you break up your reading by making up questions, reciting to yourself, and taking notes, you will learn better and find the assignment more enjoyable. In addition, changes of activity of this sort keep your mind alert and increase your absorption of material.
5. Finally, taking notes will be of immeasurable help to you later, when you review for examinations. You will seldom need to reread an entire chapter for review. If you have the contents summarized on a single notebook page, you can do a faster, more complete job of studying. You can use your textbook to refresh your memory on details not given in your notes.

TASK 1: Jot down only main facts and ideas in your preliminary outline.

Immediately after reading and reciting each section, write down the facts and ideas that you found particularly important in the preliminary outline that you developed while previewing. Your notes cannot give all the information in detail, but they can provide a clear outline. They act as cues through the key words and phrases that you have selected. These cues help you recall many of the details when you review.

Keep these four things in mind while taking notes:

1. Use key words and phrases.
2. Use your own words whenever possible. If you restate or paraphrase what you have read, you will understand and remember better.
3. Confine your notes on a chapter to one side of a notebook sheet or to two facing sheets whenever this is possible. The students who limit themselves in this manner find they can visualize more easily the relationship and arrangement of ideas. They can form a mental image of the single page or the two-page spread, and therefore they remember it better.
4. Look over your notes a day or so after you have taken them. If you discover they lack clarity, are cluttered, or are poorly organized, revise them. This will help you remember what you read. It will also make your notes more easily usable for reference and review.

Revision of notes is particularly important when a book is not well organized. If the preliminary outline you make during previewing follows a poorly arranged book, the outline is likely to be poorly arranged. If it is, you will want to revise your outline in a better form.

The discussion of previewing included an example of a preliminary outline of chapter 2 (page 30). The jottings of key words and phrases (cues) should be put directly in this outline. After you have read chapter 2, your notes may look something like the example given below.

Mastery Technique: Previewing

1. Table of Contents
        Discover: Ground covered
                       Order of topics
                       Relation of one topic to another

2. Preliminary Outline
        Record key ideas, each heading
        Look for key words; record them

3. First and Last Paragraphs
        Look in introductory paragr. for quick view of ch.
        Look in concluding paragr. for summary of ch.

4. Pictorial Aids
        Study pictures, tables, etc., for important points
        See if aids clarify important ideas

5. Inventory
        Bring together and recall what was learned from preview

Try out your notetaking skill below by making a preliminary outline for some textbook chapter you are currently reading, particularly jotting down the key words and phrases.

Your Own Example of Notes

Name of textbook _____

Title of chapter _____

Pages assigned _____

TASK 2:   Underline key words and phrases.

Many good students prefer to underline the key words in their books, at least some of the time. (This should be done, of course, only if the book belongs to you.) As in regular notetaking, just the key words should be marked. Underlining more than 15 or 20 percent of the words clutters the page and affords you little help. If you have underlined a page intelligently, weeks later you can recall the important facts by rereading only the underscored words. The following paragraph is an example of effective underlining. Note that few words, only those indicating the bare essentials, are marked.

> The <u>secondary</u> <u>schools</u> and <u>universities</u> of Poland were <u>closed</u> <u>by</u> <u>the</u> <u>Nazis</u> from the time of the invasion in 1939 until the collapse of the Nazi regime. "The Poles do not need universities or secondary schools," declared Hans Frank, the Nazi governor-general of Poland. During that six-year period many <u>teachers</u> <u>and</u> <u>professors</u>, although officially assigned to industrial or military work, continued at night <u>to</u> <u>meet</u> <u>their</u> <u>classes</u> <u>clandestinely</u> in cellars, lofts, and forests. An underground committee for education trained teachers, coordinated the teaching, and even issued diplomas. An estimated 60,000 youths were thus able to continue their secondary schooling, and approximately 6000 attended secret universities.

Read through a page from any book you own and practice taking notes by underlining. Then count the number of words you read and the number of words you underscored. Divide the number of underscored words by total words to figure the percentage of words marked.

How many words did you read? _____

How many words did you underscore? _____

About what percentage of words did you underscore? _____

TASK 3: Make diagrams to clarify ideas.

Diagrams sometimes help you to distinguish main points and fix them in your mind. A diagram of the organization of this chapter might look something like the one in example 1.

It is not always necessary to have diagrams in your notes, but they *do* give you a clear picture of groups of items that belong together. They help you to arrange facts in their correct relationship. Examples 2 and 3 summarize a large part of two reading assignments, one in English history and one in American history. The first is a family-tree diagram and the other a time-line diagram. Example 4 summarizes a reading assignment in physics.

Examples of Diagrams to Clarify Ideas

Example 1

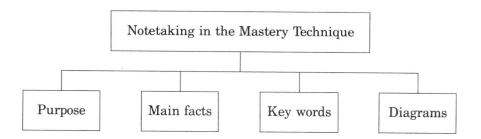

Example 2

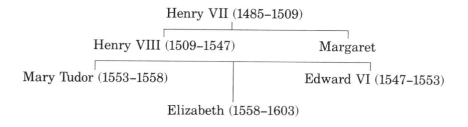

Example 3

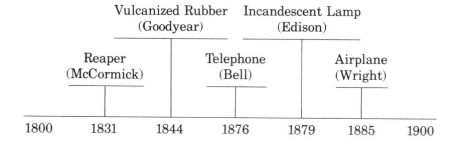

Example 4

Dispersion of Light

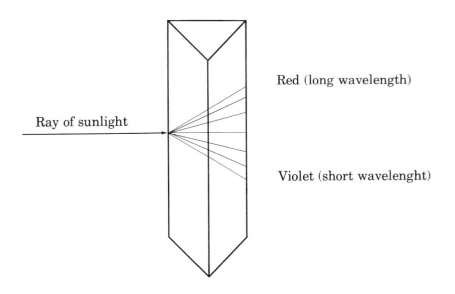

Red (long wavelength)

Ray of sunlight

Violet (short wavelenght)

Make two diagrams for a chapter you are reading now in one of your courses.

Name of book _____

Title of chapter _____

Pages assigned _____

Name of book _____

Title of chapter _____

Pages assigned _____

EXTRA PRACTICE

 Turn to the practice material on "City Planning" on page 154.
1. *Complete the preliminary outline of the selection you started in "Extra Practice" (Chapter 2); save it for "Extra Practice" in Chapter 5.*
2. *Underline key words and phrases.*
3. *Make a diagram that will simplify or clarify the selection.*
 Practice these three exercises on the material on "Latitude and Longitude" (page 156), "The Moon's Movements" (page 158), "Psychology" (page 159), and "Vitamins" (page 164).

A Bird's-Eye View of Notetaking

---

1. Jot down facts and ideas into preliminary outline.
2. Underline key words in the book if you own it.
3. Make diagrams.

5

How to Master a Textbook Chapter: REMEMBERING

The tasks you studied and practiced in the first three chapters all contribute to better remembering. Because remembering is such an important aspect of successful studying, this chapter is focused entirely on that topic. It will review and reinforce suggestions already given and will also introduce other ideas that you will find useful.

When you forget an important fact, you have lost more than just one item of information. You have also lost your power to explain and organize related information effectively. This is why forgetting details is troublesome when you are writing an examination. Examples of easily forgotten but vital details of information on two topics are given below.

After you have studied them, add examples of your own.

Subjects	Vital Facts	Facts Needed in Answering Correctly Almost Any Exam Question About:
Biology	Chromosomes are always present in pairs.	Genetics
U.S. History	France under Napoleon was feared in the United States at time of Louisiana Purchase.	Louisiana Purchase

Subjects	Vital Facts	Facts Needed in Answering Correctly Almost Any Exam Question About:

To cut down forgetting vital information, try to spend some time every day reviewing what you have learned. For more permanent recollection, base your review on the tasks described in this chapter.

Forgetting is a common experience for all of us. Experts who have studied it have discovered that students very soon forget many of the details they learned while studying an assignment. Why is so much forgotten? Can anything be done to reduce the amount of forgetting?

Consider these two facts about forgetting before we look for a solution:

1. It is easier to remember something if you are interested in it. A boy may remember batting averages of baseball players and forget important ideas in his history lesson. This is because he is interested in baseball and indifferent to history.
2. You can improve your memory. You can learn how to remember just as you can learn to play tennis or golf, if you practice the proper techniques.

What do these facts mean? Remembering can be attributed in part to intention and interest and in part to ability. If you want to remember and if you learn the skills of remembering, you will discover that your memory is far better than you realized.

TASK 1:   Find an interest in what you are studying.

Think how easily you remember an interesting experience you have had — a good book, an exciting game, an enjoyable date. The more interesting it was to you, the longer you remembered it.

Almost everyone has to study some subject that he considers dull or impractical. When you are bored with reading material in which you find little interest, try to pick out some aspect that will hold your attention. No book or subject is ever completely uninteresting. Here are some suggestions:

1. Try to find some practical use for the subject you are studying.
2. Discover at least one aspect of the subject that holds some interest for you, and study with it in mind.
3. Relate the subject to another subject in which you are already interested.
4. Think of an important reason why you should know something about the subject.

Such efforts will heighten your motivation and strengthen your intention to learn.

Name a subject you have had to study that you were bored with.

_____

_____

What particular phase of it did you find of some interest?

_____

_____

_____

Give a good reason why you should know something about the subject.

_____

_____

_____

TASK 2:   Have a clear-cut grasp of the basic ideas.

This is fundamental to good remembering. If you have only a nebulous or incomplete grasp of a topic, you will quickly forget it. The deeper your understanding, the more vivid and complete will be your remembering.

As you read this book or any book you are studying, make sure you understand each section before going on to the next. For example, if the section on previewing was not clear to you, you could not remember the ideas contained in it. You would have to understand the idea of previewing and its purpose in order to remember the other details of that chapter. Clear understanding is necessary to good remembering.

TASK 3:   Start out by getting a view of the whole.

The first step in learning is to see how the material as a whole is organized. Get an overall picture of the forest before you look at the trees. Determine what the author's main theme is and how the principal ideas are related. Then study the parts—details that support principal ideas.

Look at the headings in a chapter of a textbook you are now studying and prepare a preliminary outline based on these headings. This outline should give you a good picture of the entire chapter and of what it contains in general.

Name of textbook _____

Title of chapter _____

Preliminary Outline

Preliminary Outline (continued)

After reading some of the chapter, give an example of a detail that was clearer and more meaningful than it might have been had you not first obtained a picture of the chapter as a whole.

———————————————————————————

———————————————————————————

If something is to be memorized (a poem, a speech, or a list), the so-called "whole method" should be used if the material is not too long. The whole method consists of reading the material in its entirety over and over until it is learned. If the memory work is quite lengthy, divide it into several parts. Then read each part separately, in the correct order, until it is learned. Then recite the whole lesson.

TASK 4:   Use mnemonic devices for remembering particularly trouble-some facts.

An example of a mnemonic device is the verse "Thirty days hath September, April, June, and November . . ." that is used to recall the length of each month. The novel *Arrowsmith* tells how medical students use the verse "On old Olympus' topmost top / A fat-eared German viewed a hop" to remember the names of the twelve cranial nerves, each of which begins with the same letter as the first letter of one of the twelve words in the verse. The difference between a *stalactite* (a calcium carbonate deposit resembling an icicle hanging from the ceiling of a cavern) and a *stalagmite* (a calcium carbonate deposit on a cavern floor or ground) can be remembered by noting the letter *c* in stalactite and ceiling, and the letter *g* in stalagmite and ground.

Invent a mnemonic device for remembering something of importance in a subject you are now studying.

———————————————————————————

———————————————————————————

———————————————————————————

———————————————————————————

———————————————————————————

———————————————————————————

TASK 5:   Use more of your time in reciting than in rereading.

It would be helpful and timesaving if we could always remember what we read merely by reading. But reading alone is not enough. You need to do more than just look at the material you want to learn and remember. If you hear your own voice saying it and if you write it out and sketch diagrams of it where appropriate, you will greatly reinforce your mental image of the subject. This is because you focus all your avenues of learning (seeing, hearing, speaking, writing) upon the matter to be learned. It is all-out study.

Suppose you want to be certain to remember the eight tasks in this section on improving your memory. Recite them aloud. Have someone read them to you. Think of them while going to sleep at night, in the morning while taking a shower, or while walking to class. Test this method to see how well it works.

Reciting helps you to remember better than rereading because it forces you to think harder as you try to answer the questions you are reciting. Notetaking is written recitation. When you review your notes after finishing an assignment, try to spend most of your time in recitation – mental, oral, or written – rather than in rereading your textbook.

Begin now to recite the material covered in a current assignment, noting the time you start. Prepare notes and read the outline slowly to yourself. Then repeat as many of the details as are brought to mind by each line of notes. Turn your page of notes over and spend as much time as necessary summarizing the substance of the chapter.

Approximately how many minutes has this recitation taken? _____

Flash cards can be a great help in reciting, particularly in learning a series of facts such as the dates of historical events.

You may already be familiar with the use of flash cards in a language course. The foreign word is printed on one side of a small card and its English equivalent on the reverse. You can prepare sets of these cards yourself for various subjects. Inexpensive 3 × 5 file cards, cut in half, are handy. You can use them in history, for instance, by writing or typing an important event on one side and its date on the other, as shown on the next page.

Keep your set of drill cards, with a rubber band around them, in your pocket or handbag or tucked into a notebook or briefcase. When you have some free time, take them out and drill yourself with them. Look at the top side of the first card and try to give the information on the back. If you answer correctly, put the card away. If you don't know the information, place the card at the bottom of the pack. Continue with the second card, and so on, keeping those you know separate from those with which you are not yet completely familiar. Drill yourself on the cards you don't know.

Give examples below of facts you want to remember in a subject you are now studying.

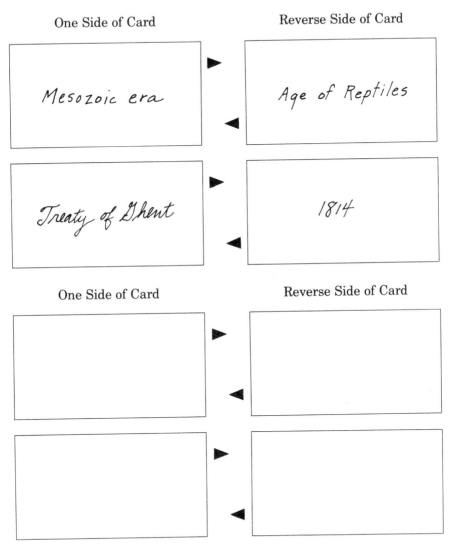

One Side of Card   Reverse Side of Card

Mesozoic era   *Age of Reptiles*

Treaty of Ghent   *1814*

One Side of Card   Reverse Side of Card

TASK 6: Distribute your practice in learning over several study periods.

You will remember more of an assignment if you divide your study time into several separate sessions. Distribute your study of any subject over two or more periods of moderate length. Don't try to learn the whole assignment in one long continuous period if you can avoid it. After fatigue sets in, practice does not produce good or permanent learning.

Psychologists have discovered that time is required for an idea to ripen in the mind. Time spaces between periods of studying an assignment allow the ideas to ripen by the time you have finished studying them. Ripe ideas remain; unripe ideas leave your mind quickly.

Many things you will want to remember indefinitely — not just until examination time. Spaced practice is the answer. First, practice at frequent intervals (if only by reciting or recalling what you want to remember). Then practice — indefinitely — at longer intervals.

Let's see how task 6 applies to your reading of this chapter. You might pore over it for several additional hours today. But you will achieve more if you come back to it again tomorrow and again the next day. Your plan might be to read the chapter today, then review and recite the mastery technique tomorrow and the next day.

TASK 7: Do part of your studying with others.

The bulk of your studying should be done alone. When working by yourself, you can concentrate on those points of an assignment that are particularly difficult for *you.*

There are, however, several benefits that come from collaborating with one or two fellow students for part of your studying. The exchange of ideas with friends can be a stimulating experience. It is close to conversation, broadening your interests and interpretations and deepening your understanding of the subject.

With an "audience" of one or two others, you are forced to recite fully and in detail in order that the others will understand you and be able to react to what you are saying. When it comes their turn to recite, you, as a listener, will continue to recite, in a sense, by hearing the others speak.

Become part of a small group of fellow students to recite the contents of a reading assignment.

Nature of the assignment _____

_____

Describe your procedure and evaluate its benefit.

_____

_____

TASK 8:   Learn for the future.

If you memorize something only well enough to pass an examination, you will probably forget it quickly. If a fact or idea is worth learning at all, it is usually worth retaining.

Psychologists have discovered that you can learn for the future if you continue to memorize after you have first reached mastery. One psychologist, for example, had students learn a list of nouns. He tested their retention of the words over a period of twenty-eight days. Those who spent considerable time memorizing them after mastery remembered four times as many nouns as did those who stopped memorizing when they had achieved mastery.

Make it a habit to continue to learn something after you feel you have completed the learning. If you are studying Spanish, for instance, and finish an assignment that consists of learning a list of words or rules, spend extra time on them. You will learn them better and they will remain with you longer.

Take an assignment you are now working with that requires straight memorization. Time yourself from the moment you begin until you can say, "I have learned the material."

Subject _____

Nature of assignment _____

_____

Length of time required _____

Now spend from one-fourth to one-half of that time in additional learning of the same material. This is what is involved in learning for the future.

You can fix ideas in the mind as well as lists, rules, formulas, and the like by practicing them beyond mastery. You can practice by explaining the ideas to a friend or by talking about them in a conversation.

Another method that is extremely useful in learning for the future consists of integrating what you once learned (yesterday, last month, or even last year) with what you are learning today. For example, suppose that in biology early in the year you learned about the mutually beneficial relation between diverse organisms inhabiting a particular environment. The relationship of the beech tree and a certain fungus was cited as an illustration. Later on in the course you read in a chapter on the fungi that certain fungi live in the soil as parasites on the roots of plants and make it possible for the root to absorb necessary minerals. You should then recall the earlier treatment of interrelationships of organisms, and consciously integrate that information with the new information.

Such integration often takes place between different subjects. For example, you tie in the information you gained in a science course about infectious diseases with an account in a history course of the successful battle against yellow fever that paved the way for the construction of the Panama Canal. When you place old learning in a new setting in such a manner, you are helping tremendously to fix it in your mind.

EXTRA PRACTICE

Turn to the practice material on "City Planning" on page 154.

1. *State in writing what part or parts of the selection are of special interest to you. If you cannot honestly find an interest, state why the subject is important, or state some practical use of the subject.*

2. *Refer to the outline you made of this selection in "Extra Practice," exercise 1, on page 55. Read it over several times until you get a clear, firm picture of the whole selection.*

3. *Invent a mnemonic device that would be useful in remembering the selection's main points.*

4. *Recite the content by saying it first to yourself, then to a friend, and finally by writing it.*

5. *Now learn it for the future by continuing to study it "beyond mastery."*

Practice these three exercises on the material on "Latitude and Longitude (page 156), "The Moon's Movements" (page 158), "Psychology" (page 159), and "Vitamins" (page 164).

A Bird's-Eye View of Remembering

1. Find an interest.
2. Grasp basic ideas.
3. Get view of whole.
4. Use mnemonic devices.
5. Recite.
6. Distribute your study time.
7. Study part of time with others.
8. Learn for future.

THE MASTERY TECHNIQUE SUMMED UP

Chapters 2 through 5 are the most important ones in this book. Now that you have read them, you should possess the secrets of study know-how. If you can begin to combine the mastery technique of previewing, reading, notetaking, and remembering in your studying, you are headed toward becoming master of your assignments. You will also be more interested in your assignments, and this will speed up your studying and make it more pleasant for you.

You learn to swim by swimming, not by reading about swimming. In learning to study, you will master the technique of studying by applying the ideas in this book, not simply by reading about them. By performing the tasks of the mastery technique as you do your assignments in your subjects, you can learn to study efficiently.

If you use the mastery technique, you will save hours of time. Many students have cut their study time in half by using it.

Are you sure you understand the mastery technique and know how to use it in your daily assignments? If not, go back and study the parts you are not sure of before going on to the additional study methods in the following chapters.

6

How to Listen More Effectively

Listening, like reading, is a way of learning both in and out of school. You can learn in class, for example, by listening to your instructor's explanations and to class discussions, as well as by reading your text.

There is a good deal more to listening than just hearing sounds. Good listening, like good reading, is an active process. The good listener is constantly thinking, evaluating, and making connections.

Tests show that many students actually miss about half of the main ideas and about three out of five of the details while listening. Why do they miss so much? In part, because they do not understand the ideas presented. But many students have trouble because they have not developed the skills of listening.

These skills are study skills. You can make substantial improvement as a student by improving as a listener.

During our lives most of us listen about three times as much as we read. Did you ever stop to think how much you listen to people talking every day? You listen to your family, friends, and other people at home, on the street, in stores; you listen on the telephone, to the radio and to television, and in consultations with teachers, doctors, and dentists; you may listen to sermons on Sunday, to dialogues in movies and plays, to talks at meetings.

When you take a job, you have to listen to instructions from your employer and to discussions and reports by co-workers. Your job depends on it: how well you listen may affect your progress in your work.

You have found out already how important good listening is in social life and in family living. You know how disturbing it can be when someone fails to give undivided attention in conversation and is unable to contribute when addressed.

When in class, you have to absorb everything that is said. Your instructors and classmates will present material and explanations that you may not find in your textbooks. You cannot always rely on the help of your friends for some point of information you have missed in class. No one else can listen for you. Improving your listening habits and skills will improve all of your schoolwork.

Better listening will also enlarge your vocabulary because you will hear new words and learn how they are used. You are probably aware that you often learn new words by hearing them spoken.

While good listening is very useful, it is not always easy. Here are seven major reasons why good listening is difficult:

1. The speaker's pace may not be yours. When listening, you have to travel mentally at the speed of the person who is speaking, rather than at your own. The speaker may talk too rapidly for you to take in everything that is being said. Or the speaker may talk so slowly that between the words or phrases your mind wanders, and you find it hard to concentrate on what he or she is saying.

2. You cannot choose the time and place for listening. You often have to adjust your mood and your power of concentration to difficult situations. If you had a headache while reading a book on your own time, you could put it aside until you felt better. But you cannot do that during a class discussion or lecture. You have to absorb as much information as you can, even if you are ill.

3. There may be distractions in the classroom. Perhaps you are interested in some member of the opposite sex sitting near you. Or a friend may pass a note or whisper a bit of news to you or to a neighbor. Your attention wanders from the speaker, and you miss something important. You may have a hard time catching the thread of the talk again. The very presence of others in the room makes it hard for some people to concentrate.

4. A lecture, discussion, or conversation is a fleeting thing. What is said one moment is gone the next. You do not have time to recite it as the talk unwinds. You cannot play the words over again like a phonograph record (unless you use a tape recorder) or turn back the pages of a conversation like the pages of a book. If you do not comprehend as it is spoken, you have missed it.

5. You should evaluate what is presented to you for learning, but it is hard to be as critical as you should be when you are listening.

Unless the speaker takes long pauses, you will not have much time for judging the value, the importance, and the truth of what you hear.

6. A speaker's personality and delivery may throw you off guard. If a speaker sounds unsure of himself or herself, for example, you might conclude that he or she does not know the subject. Yet the speaker may be presenting valuable information. So take it all in and reserve your judgment until later.

7. The reaction of others to the speaker may prove contagious. You may find yourself influenced by classmates' reactions and consequently arrive at a false judgment of the speaker or the material. Whether favorable or unfavorable, this false judgment may keep you from understanding and properly evaluating what the speaker is saying.

These are some of the main difficulties of efficient listening in class. But do not be discouraged. You can train yourself to be a good listener by practicing the tasks described in the succeeding pages of this chapter. You will find it definitely worth your while to listen well both now and after you are out of school.

TASK 1:   Prepare for listening.

When you know the subject of a lecture or discussion in advance, you can prepare to get the most out of it in two ways: (1) review what you already know about the subject and (2) read as much more about it as you can. Even a little background will give you an idea of what the speaker is talking about and will make it easier to listen. Having geared yourself to the general topic, you will not be totally uninformed at the beginning of the lecture or discussion.

For example, suppose your instructor has planned a discussion on the work of the United States Supreme Court. You remember that it is the highest judicial body in our government, and that it sometimes makes final decisions on the constitutionality of laws passed by Congress. To sharpen your recollection and extend your knowledge, you read a few pages about it from a book on history or government. You learn among other things that it was Chief Justice John Marshall who, early in the nineteenth century, established the right of the Supreme Court to make final decisions concerning laws of a state legislature or of Congress.

In class your instructor might refer to Marshall as having strengthened the federal government, without clearly explaining how. But you would know because you did some preparation. There would be no need for you to pause in your listening to wonder and perhaps to miss the lecturer's next point. Nor would you have to sit through the rest of the discussion in confusion because of your ignorance.

If you have looked over the subject matter in advance, you are not likely to be upset by the speaker's use of technical terms. If, for example, a speaker uses the phrase *judicial review* without explaining its meaning, you will know what he or she is talking about if you have done some preparatory reading.

If you are somewhat familiar with the subject, in other words, you can concentrate more easily on the lecture even in a difficult listening situation. You are able to keep pace mentally with the speaker, absorb more readily what is said, retain what you hear longer, and take notes more easily. In short, you can listen intelligently.

Make a plan for preparing for a lecture or class discussion that you will hear in the next few days.

Subject _____

_____

Topic that will be talked about _____

_____

_____

_____

Books you have located in which you plan to do some reading:

Title	Chapters or pages

TASK 2:   While listening, search for main ideas.

Try to determine from the very beginning of a lecture, discussion, or conference where the speaker is headed. What is Professor Black's purpose? What ideas is he trying to develop? Any background you have acquired in preparation for the lecture should help you answer these questions. From the moment he starts to speak, concentrate on finding his main ideas.

Sometimes a speaker will assist you by listing the main points at the beginning of his talk. For example, in discussing the camera lens, the instructor might say: "I am going to describe a good camera lens by telling about its four most important attributes. These are, first, focal length; second, speed; third, resolving power; and fourth, depth of field." At the end of the talk, the speaker may summarize each of these four points. If this happens, you are fortunate. You do not have to hunt through all his statements for the main ideas.

When your instructor does not give you a clue about the number and content of the main points, you may have a hard time sifting them out. This process requires skill that takes practice. You have to pay particularly close attention. You may not be able to select the main ideas until later, when you go over your notes. At the end of class you may want to compare your list of main points with those of other students to make sure you obtained them all.

During a lecture do not be sidetracked by irrelevant details such as humorous illustrations, odd expressions, new words, or single fascinating but unimportant facts. Remember what you can of them for background information, but always keep in mind the main ideas. They are the meat of the subject and of future examinations.

When you go to a class lecture, make up your mind to look first for main ideas. You probably have an indication of what some of these points will be from your advance preparation. Listen for phrases that will guide you, such as "First of all . . ."; "Nothing is more significant than . . ."; "The reason for this is . . ."; "Above all, do not forget that . . ."; "Next in importance is . . ."

Second, practice catching and sorting out main ideas in class discussions and lectures whenever you have the chance. Practice, too, with something easier such as a radio or television talk on a subject with which you are familiar.

List the main ideas you recall from a recent listening situation.

The occasion (Where? When? What?)

_____

_____

The main ideas _____

_____

_____

_____

_____

_____

_____

Give an example of a lecture you have heard, from which you remember only a humorous story or some unusual incident but have forgotten the main points.

_____

_____

_____

_____

_____

_____

_____

TASK 3:   While listening, take notes.

You have prepared for class by doing some reading. You have concentrated carefully on everything the instructor said, and you have tried to pick out the main ideas. Now you will want to keep a record of those ideas you have worked so hard to obtain. Taking notes gives you a permanent record.

Notes are better than a reference book that can be used only in the library or a borrowed book that must be returned. Your notes are your property. They will be your guide at examination time. A good set of notes is the best source of review.

Taking notes forces you to concentrate on what is being said. If you are determined to take notes, you must fix your attention on the speaker. Your notes also will provide a means for evaluating what you hear. You can study them later for this purpose.

Your notes will not be of much use to you if they are not as complete as you can make them. All the main points and important details should go into them. In order to take really usable notes, try to write down the following four items when listening to a talk:

1. Main ideas
2. Key points under main ideas
3. Specific words, names, figures of speech, dates, and other data that seem important
4. Any important words whose meanings you are not sure of

It is not as easy to take orderly notes while listening as while reading. You have to do two things at once: you have to write down what has been said and at the same time listen to the succeeding points. This is particularly hard if the speaker has not defined main ideas clearly, or frequently wanders from the subject. But you have one advantage over the speaker: you can think faster than he or she can speak. This gives you time not only to take notes but to think back and to think ahead while doing so. By taking full advantage of this time difference, you can learn to make each note a solid bridge between what was just said and what seems to be coming. This is the secret of clear notes.

Go to your next class prepared to take notes, keeping the above four points in mind. Take advantage of every opportunity for notetaking. Let radio, television, club meetings, debates, bull sessions, and telephone conversations serve as your training field.

Of course you cannot always take notes. But if you practice taking them in reasonable situations, you will become not only a better notetaker but a better listener. You will get into the habit of listening for main ideas whether or not you are in a position to take notes.

Study the class notes below, taken down by a male student. Note that the listener circled words of whose meanings he was not sure. Note also his shorthand—"nec" for necessary, *"w" for* with, *"fr" for* from, *and the like.*

**Example of Lecture Notes (Before Revision)
Taken During a Lecture on Forestry**

The Value of Forests

Formerly forests had negative value
    Were something to be conquered
    Removal nec for clearing for houses, farmland

Wood now recogd most needed and used prod of nature
    Use from cradle to coffin
    Houses, furniture, tools, paper, bks, etc.

Other uses
    Maple sugar, nuts, fruit, tanning materials, charcoal, wood alcohol, etc.

Other values of forests: soil enrichment, soil holding, flood prvntion, pannage,
    wildlife refuges, beautific'n

Value of trees (which are not part of forest)
    Shade, ornamt, windbreaks, screen unsightly objects, frame views
    Thous $ spent by park & home owners ea yr

Example of valuable genus - oak
    Distrib't over temperate climates of world & all kinds of habitats
    Wood — strong, hard
    Bark & galls - rich in tannin
    Nuts — food for swine; roasted for coffee subst
    Ex of oak — white oak — wood most valuable of all oaks
    Wt. — 46 lb per cu ft
    Uses — RR ties, bldg constr (exterior & interior), ship bldg, tool handles

Qs after lecture
    Q — White oak 46 lb per cu ft
        How compare w other wood?
    A — White oak considered heavy
        Compare w white pine's 24 lb
    Q — If white pine so light, why so much used?
    A — Wood does not have to be strong & hard to be usefl. Wh pine soft,
        easily worked & has uses oak doesn't
    Q — How much forestland in US?
    A — About $\frac{1}{2}$ billion acres, mostly in private hands

*Now, below, record an example of your notes taken during a class talk,
lecture, or discussion. Make up your own brief forms as you go along.*

Example of Your Own Notes from a Lecture or Discussion (Before Revision)

TASK 4:   Revise notes later.

Unless the lecture is exceptionally well-organized, your notes will not be in ideal order. Speaking is often informal and full of idle backtracking and illogical arrangement of subjects. You do not have time to sort out and mentally rearrange the material as you jot down your notes.

Suppose a lecturer says, "I meant to say before that. . . ." You don't have time to look back for the right place to insert this afterthought; you must simply jot it down as the next note. Then you should insert it later in its proper place.

No matter how good a listener or notetaker you are, you are bound to emerge from many classes with jumbled notes. In this shape they are hardly satisfactory for permanent use. You would be wasting time if you tried to use them in such rough condition for reference or review. They need to be reworked and rearranged on a fresh sheet of notebook paper.

The sooner after class you can go over your notes and revise them, the easier and more quickly you can clarify them. The material ought to be fresh as possible in your mind. There may be omissions in your notes that you can supply from memory if you do not wait until the cues are stale. Revision of your notes may be a nuisance, but it has real value.

1. You clear up points you may not have understood. As you rearrange your notes, you are forced to think them through. In so doing, a new or complicated idea may become clear.
2. You fix the material more firmly in your mind for future use. Rethinking and reworking are forms of recitation.
3. You have an orderly, usable record for later reference and review.

Here is a revision of the original notes on forests from page 76.

The Value of Forests

Forest Products
> Wood (one of most needed and widely used prods of nature):

Construction	Books
Furniture	Charcoal
Tools	Wood alcohol
Paper	

Products Other than Wood

| Fruit | Bark (tannin) |
| Nuts | Sap (maple) |

Forest Uses Other than Products

Soil holding & flood control	Wildlife refuge
Soil improvement (humus)	Beauty
Pannage for swine	Recreation area

Uses of Trees that Are Not Members of Forest
   Shade   Screen the unsightly
   Ornament   Frame a view
   Windbreaks

Oak – Example of a Valuable Forest Tree
   Distributed over temperate climates of world and all kinds of habitats
   Strong, hard wood, e.g., white oak esp. valuable – hard (46 lb per cu ft) –
      used for RR ties, construction & finish, ship bldg, tool handles
   But wood does not have to be strong, hard & heavy to be useful; e.g.,
      white pine only 24 lb per cu ft & has many uses
   Nuts (swine and coffee)
   Bark & galls (tannin)

Definition of Words
   Pannage – Food found by swine in forest (acorns, hickory nuts, etc.)
   Windbreak – Group of trees providing shelter from wind
   Genus – A subdivision of family; oaks are a genus belonging to beech
      family
   Habitat – Place where a plant or animal is usually found
   Gall – Swelling on a plant caused by certain insects
   Tannin – Substance used in tanning and dyeing

Here are some suggestions for revising your own notes.

First, review your notes and cross out any items that you decide are not really important. For instance, "used from cradle to coffin" in the example on page 76 could be omitted in a revision as unimportant in the study of forests.

Underscore the main points in your notes if you did not do so during class. (These points will stand out better if underscored in pencil or ink of a different color from that of your notes.)

Next, rework your notes to arrange the material in logical outline form. Your object is to assemble under the correct heading all material that belongs together. Note in the example on page 76 and above how all material has been grouped under six main headings. All products have been brought together under two headings; all other uses of forest and trees are grouped under two other headings. Two additional main headings have been used to include illustration and clarification: "Oak – Example of a Valuable Forest Tree" and "Definition of Words."

You may want to break up the notes under a main heading into two or more groups, supplying subheadings where necessary. Keep the outline simple, but include all important material. A simple outline will be easier to study than a detailed, complicated one.

In your revision, use your own words in place of the instructor's words wherever possible. This is a check on your understanding of the subject.

Go over the instructor's answers to questions from the class (listed at the end of your notes), and work this information into your revision where it logically belongs. In the sample revision you will find that answers to questions on the oak tree have been included with lecture material on the oak.

During the lecture you circled all words whose meanings were not clear. Now consult the dictionary and list these words and their definitions at the end of your newly outlined notes, as in the example. Knowing their exact meanings will improve your understanding of the subject, and listing them makes them available for review and reference.

If your notes are logically organized, simply outlined, and brief, you will be delighted with the ease and speed with which you can review them when you want to. You may find that you already remember many facts better because you were actually reciting as you thought them through and reworked them. Thus your reviewing time should be cut down even more.

Following these suggestions, revise your notes on a fresh sheet of notebook paper in their new outline form as your permanent record of the class session. Leave space under each heading for approximately the amount of detail you estimate will go there. Then list the detail as briefly and succinctly as possible under the right headings.

**Your Notes Revised
(Revision of Notes Given on Page 77)**

Your Notes Revised (continued)

Review Exercise

Prepare for an actual lecture or discussion that you know will take place in one of your classes within the next few days.

Subject, problem, or question that will be taken up _____

_____

Type of meeting (lecture, discussion, conference, or other) _____

Time schedule (date and hours) _____

Summarize what you already know about the subject to be discussed.

_____

_____

_____

_____

_____

Find a book on the subject that would be helpful in preparing you for the meeting. List the author, title, and date of publication of the book.

_____

_____

Portion of book that applies (chapter or pages) _____

Read the above portion of the book and summarize the background it gives you.

_____

_____

During the meeting, take notes below; or take them on a separate sheet of paper and copy them on the following page at a later time.

**Copy of Original Notes
(Review Exercise)**

After you have attended the meeting, answer the following questions.

List the main ideas developed by the speaker or speakers during the meeting.

_____

_____

_____

_____

_____

_____

Did you encounter any difficulties in determining the main ideas? What were the listening problems and how did you solve them?

_____

_____

_____

_____

_____

_____

_____

Revise your notes, using either the following page or a separate sheet from which you will copy them here at a later date.

**Copy of Revised Notes
(Review Exercise)**

EXTRA PRACTICE

Turn to the mini-lecture, "Foreign Trade," on page 166. Arrange a listening practice session with a few of your classmates. Have one of the group read it as a lecture. This means it should be read at the rate of delivery and with the expressiveness of a good lecturer. The rest of you take notes. After the mini-lecture, take ten minutes to revise them.

Compare one another's notes.

1. To what extent do the group's revised notes agree in content? In form?
2. Which sets of notes would be the best for preparing for an exam? What features make them the best?

Repeat, having another member of your group read the mini-lecture, "Changes in Agriculture," on page 167.

A Bird's-Eye View of Listening More Effectively

1. Prepare for listening.
2. While listening, look for main ideas.
3. While listening, take notes.
4. Revise notes later.

7

How to Prepare
for Examinations

Your best preparation for examinations is regular day-by-day study. If you apply the skills described in the preceding chapters, you will study for exams as you go along. You will be reciting and reviewing. You will not wait to begin reviewing until the night or even the week before exams. You prepare for them all term as you study your daily assignments.

If you follow the suggestions in the earlier chapters, the results will show in your exams. But you will still have to solve the problem of recalling, late in a semester, what you covered at the beginning. If you leave this material until exam time, you will have to relearn much of it. Instructors sometimes help with periodic reviews. But your job as a student is to reserve time to look over your textbooks and notes from earlier portions of the course. Do this one day a month.

In addition to monthly reviews, it is always advisable to do some special review work immediately before exams. The following pages will show you how to take your exams in stride.

TASK 1: Plan a definite examination study schedule and stick to it.

You will need to modify your study schedule for the week or two-week period preceding a major exam and for one or two days preceding a minor quiz.

This special preparation is worthwhile. It will save you from frenzied last-minute cramming and will make you more relaxed and confident at exam time.

Make up your schedule to show the exact days and hours for your pre-exam studying in each course. The following suggestions may help.

1. Plan for exam preparation periods of at least one-half hour.
2. Distribute your study time for a particular subject over at least two sessions in studying for minor exams and over at least three sessions in studying for major ones. Do not depend solely on eleventh-hour cramming!

Now construct a schedule to serve you when your next examination period arrives.

Your Exam Study Schedule

Subject	Day	Hour

TASK 2: Prepare and study a master outline of the subject.

During the first exam study period make a master outline of the material you have dealt with in the subject. A master outline is a condensed version of all your notes. It combines class notes on lectures and discussions, notes you made when reading your textbook, and notes from your supplementary reading.

The act of making a master outline is in itself an excellent review. When you have finished the outline, read it over as often as you can before the exam. Recite to yourself the facts and ideas related to each item in the outline.

Study the example of a master outline at the end of this paragraph. It was made up for an examination in a course on study methods and covers the subject matter of the first four chapters of this book. Notice its informality—abbreviations and the use of strokes to indicate "of," "for," and "by." Each student usually works out his or her own shorthand devices.

Example of Master Outline in Preparation for an Examination

Exam in course on study skills covering introduction and chapters 1 through 4 of this book.

Introduction. Advntgs effcnt study
    A. Quality/work
    B. Enjoyment
    C. Time/leisure
    D. Composure
Mastery Tech
    A. Previewing
        1. Sets stage
        2. Forest before trees
        3. Rules
            (a) Table/contents
            (b) Headings
            (c) First, last parag
            (d) Pix, etc.
            (e) Invntry

    B. Reading
        1. What is it?
            (a) Thinking
            (b) Anticipating
        2. Rules for vocab
            (a) Spot
            (b) Context
            (c) Dictionary
            (d) Record
            (e) Use
        3. Rules for Q-reading
            (a) Headings→Qs
            (b) Look/answs
            (c) Recite answs
            (d) Reread

    C. Notes
        1. Purposes
            (a) Overview
            (b) Keeps alert
            (c) Review for exams
        2. Rules
            (a) Main facts/ideas
            (b) Key wds
            (c) Diagrams

    D. Memory
        1. Causes/forgetting
           (a) Lack/intrst
           (b) Lack/skills
        2. Rules
           (a) Take intrst
           (b) Understnd
           (c) Learn/wholes
           (d) Recite
           (e) Key wds
           (f) Many senses
           (g) Distrbut time
           (h) Future use
           (i) Apply

Use your own kind of shorthand as a timesaver in drawing up a chapter outline. Try to keep it to one page, that is, to one side of a sheet, or to two facing pages.

TASK 3: Make up an examination, as if you were the instructor, for each course in which you expect to be tested; then take the examination.

Ask your instructor whether he or she plans to give an essay exam or an objective exam.

An essay exam is one that requires written discussion in answer to its questions. You have to supply the facts, organize them in logical order, and write them up in a well-rounded essay. Creative thinking, ability to organize, and careful writing are necessary in order to do well on an essay exam. You also have to understand main ideas and remember detailed related facts.

An objective exam asks for bare facts and is made up of different types of questions: true-false, multiple choice, matching, and sentence completion. It requires little writing. It tests mainly the ability to recognize true statements of facts and concepts.

Since the essay exam and the objective exam are answered in entirely different ways, it is helpful to know which kind of exam will be given. Let us first look at the problem of essay exams.

Here are some of the things an essay question might ask you to do, with examples of questions and answers.

    A. **Compare:** to find similarities and differences between two or more things.

Question: Compare the planets Earth and Mars.

Answer: (While this question would usually be answered in one or more paragraphs, it will be answered below in chart form in order to show in a more clear-cut fashion what is involved in making a comparison.)

Characteristics	Earth	Mars
shape	approximately spherical	approximately spherical
diameter	approximately 8000 mi.	approximately 4000 mi.
rotation	approximately once in 24 hr.	approximately once in $24\frac{1}{2}$ hr.
revolution	approximately once in 12 mo.	approximately once in 23 mo.
surface	relatively uneven	relatively flat
distance from sun	approximately 93,000,000 mi.	approximately 140,000,000 mi.

B. Contrast: to find differences between two or more things.

Question: Contrast Latin America with Anglo America.

Answer: (Again, while such a question would usually be answered in one or more paragraphs, it will be answered below in chart form to illustrate the contrast in a more clear-cut fashion.)

Characteristics	Latin America	Anglo America
origin	military conquest	colonization by free people
climate	largely tropical	temperate
industrialization	restricted	advanced
European cultural influences	comparatively strong	comparatively weak
religion	comparatively uniform	diverse
compulsory education	wide range of standards	comparatively uniform

C. Define: to set forth the meaning. It is a good idea to follow a definition with an example.

Question: Define the term *figure of speech*

Answer: A figure of speech is an expression in which words are used in other than their literal meaning. For example: "France was swept off her feet by Hitler's army."

D. Describe: to give an account of.

Question: Describe in one sentence Stephen Crane's *Red Badge of Courage.*

Answer: *The Red Badge of Courage* is a novel of the Civil War
that vividly describes the ordeal under gunfire of its
hero, a young recruit.

E. **List:** to record a series of things such as words, names, or
facts. The items should appear below one another in
list form.

Question: List three causes of discontent among the colonists
that contributed to the American Revolution.

Answer: 1. The Proclamation of 1763, which confined land
settlements east of the Appalachians
2. The Sugar Act of 1764, which taxed trade between
the colonies and the West Indies
3. The Stamp Act of 1765, which taxed newspapers
and documents of various kinds

F. **Explain:** to state fully and interpret clearly details pertaining
to an incident.

Question: Explain why the United States did not join the League
of Nations.

Answer: The many American isolationists of the period following World War I disliked the League's Article Ten,
which authorized military and economic sanctions
against any nation resorting to war. This looked to
them to be risky entanglement in Europe's troubles.
Certain Republican leaders opposed the League, in
part at least, to discredit the Democrats.

G. **Illustrate:** to make clear by giving an example.

Question: Illustrate a balanced diet.

Answer: Meat and cheese for protein, potatoes and bread for
carbohydrates, milk and butter for fats, fresh fruits
and vegetables for vitamins and minerals, and water.

H. **Outline:** to summarize by a series of headings and subheadings.

Question: Outline the steps preceding the actual writing of a
resource theme.

Answer: I. Collect information on the subject.
   A. Record data on index cards.
   B. Group cards into categories representing sec-
      tions of the theme.

II. Draft an outline.
   A. List the points in proposed order of treatment.
   B. Use numbers, letters, and indentations to show the rank of each point.

When you make and take your own essay exam for practice, it is not necessary to take time to write the answers in full. It is enough to outline the answers informally, using phrases instead of sentences. Here is an example of an essay question and how you might informally outline the answer:

Question: Why does the sea play a larger part in the life of the people of Norway than in the life of the people of other European countries?

Answer: No other European country has such unfavorable terrain

Most of Norway unproductive

Arable surface but 2 percent of area

N. Atlantic Drift makes for mild year-round climate

Harbors open when those of neighboring countries (such as Swedish ports in the Gulf of Bothnia) are closed

Numerous deep fjords provide calm water cradles for training sailors

Sites for fishing villages

Norwegians therefore turn to sea for food and trade

Large, modern fishing and whaling fleets, merchant marine, etc.

Prepare an essay examination covering a course or subject you are now taking.

Your question that requires:	*Your brief answer*
comparison	
contrast	
definition	
description	

Your question that requires:	*Your brief answer*
listing	
explanation	
illustration	
outlining	

Let us now see what an objective examination is like. Instead of questions, the test usually consists of statements to be marked true or false, to complete, or to match with other given items.

One objective examination may consist of several varieties of these questions. It is well to be prepared to answer all types. Samples of the most common types of objective questions are given:

True-false questions

Directions: Circle T if item is true and F if item is false.

Example: T F   Since 1949 Siam has been known officially as Thailand.

Multiple-choice questions

Directions: Place the letter of the correct answer on the blank line.

Example: ____ Most physical forces are electromagnetic in origin, but an important exception is
a. gravitational force
b. frictional force
c. cohesive force
d. chemical force

Matching questions

Directions: Match the items in the left-hand column with those in the right-hand column by placing the appropriate letter on the blank line.

Example: ____ Hyperbole   a. A figure of speech comparing two unlike things.

____ Simile   b. An extreme exaggeration

_____ Metaphor c. A word or phrase used in place of another to suggest a likeness between them

_____ Antitheses d. Opposing or contrasting ideas

         e. Any figure of speech

Completion questions

  Directions: Place on the blank line the word or words that will correctly complete the sentence.

  Example: The ruling sovereigns of ancient Egypt were called _____

Construct an objective examination for a course or subject you are now taking.

True-false (3 items)

T F 1. _____

     _____

T F 2. _____

     _____

T F 3. _____

     _____

Multiple-choice (3 items)

_____ 4. _____

     _____

    a. _____

    b. _____

    c. _____

_____ 5. _____

     _____

a. _____

b. _____

c. _____

_____   6. _____

_____

a. _____

b. _____

c. _____

Matching (3 matched pairs)

_____   7. _____   a. _____

_____   _____

8. _____   b. _____

_____   _____

_____   9. _____   c. _____

_____   _____

Completion (3 items)

10. _____

_____

11. _____

_____

12. _____

_____

When you have completed the test, check with your notes and textbook to see if you have included all pertinent points. Then answer your test questions.

TASK 4:   Pay special attention to troublesome points.

The preceding task will help you find your weak spots. Make a list of the hard-to-remember and troublesome points and work on them. You can record them on flash cards like those described in chapter 5.

Whether you use a list or cards, your job is to review these troublesome points by reciting them from memory either silently or aloud, or by writing them. If you have time, use all three methods on each point until you are sure you will not forget it.

What are some of the troublesome points revealed by the exam you constructed and took?

_____

_____

_____

_____

_____

_____

Practice reciting them.

TASK 5:   Cram as the last step.

If you have ever crammed frantically most of the night for an exam, as most of us have at one time or another, you may have felt that you had made a mistake in leaving your studying until the last minute. And so you had. If you stay up much later than usual, you might not be fit to take the exam. Then why do we tell you to cram? Because cramming just before an exam can be helpful as a final review of material that you have studied and reviewed. If cramming follows the other tasks suggested in this chapter, it is psychologically sound and will help you to remember your material. For many students, however, cramming is the only technique employed in studying for examinations; this kind of cramming results in superficial learning. When the exam is over, the disconnected knowledge jammed into your mind at the last minute quickly disappears.

Cram the last day and evening before an exam, therefore, to clinch the more troublesome points in the material you have been reviewing. Then go to bed at your usual time so that your mind will be clear for the examination.

EXTRA PRACTICE

Prepare for an examination on "Psychology" beginning on page 159. (You will take a "Psychology" quiz following your study of the next chapter.)

Now prepare for an exam on "Vitamins" beginning on page 164, keeping in mind that you will take a real quiz on that material following your study of the next chapter.

A Bird's-Eye View of
Getting Ready for Examinations

1. Develop an examination study schedule.
2. Make and study a master outline.
3. Make up an examination for each subject and take your examination.
4. Pay special attention to troublesome points.
5. Cram.

8

How to Take Examinations

Up to this point we have discussed how to prepare for exams. If you apply the tasks outlined in the first section of this book, you should be able to go to your exam confident that you know your subject and free from the sinking sensation that comes from being half-prepared.

But knowing your subject is only part of your examination job. You also have to know how to write examinations. There are several things you can do that may make the difference between a fair mark and a good or excellent one. Some of these concern getting started, making a wise choice of questions, organizing your answers, and catching careless errors.

WRITING ESSAY EXAMINATIONS

TASK 1: Underline important words in the directions.

It is extremely important to follow directions exactly. Before you write anything, read the whole exam carefully, making sure you understand every question, and underline the key words in the directions and questions. This will direct your attention to important words, focus your thinking on the exam, clear your mind, and get you off to a good start. It will prevent your trying to write before you are settled and organized. If there is something you do not understand, ask the instructor to clarify it for you. Do not begin writing until you understand all directions and questions.

Often an exam will contain more questions than you are expected to answer. You are given several choices. If you do not read the directions carefully, you may try to answer all the questions. Then you will probably not have time to answer any of them adequately, and you may lose points on your grade.

Suppose that an exam contains ten questions and directs you to answer any three. To make sure you do not answer them all, underline the words *any three* in the directions like this:

Answer <u>any three</u> of the following questions.

Underline similarly significant words in the following directions.

(a) *Answer the first two questions and one other question.*

(b) *Answer the first question in full and answer the other questions in outline form.*

(c) *Answer questions 1, 2, and 3 in detail and questions 4 and 5 briefly.*

(d) *Answer the following two questions and one that you make up yourself.*

Look at this example of an exam question in which the important words are underlined.

<u>Compare</u> rereading and reciting <u>as</u> <u>methods</u> <u>of</u> <u>improving</u> <u>recall</u>.

The word *compare* is important. It means to find similarities and differences. Note further in the above question that rereading and reciting are not to be compared in general, but only "as methods of improving recall." Make sure you do exactly what a question asks. If you do not, your instructor may feel you do not know the answer and are evading or bluffing. Underlining can help avoid this embarrassment and misunderstanding.

TASK 2:   Outline the answer to each essay question.

Answer the easiest question first. Begin by jotting down key words and phrases to make an informal outline of your proposed answer. Do not make it formal or detailed. Use the question sheet, scratch paper if permitted by your instructor, or the inside covers of your exam booklet for this purpose.

Try outlining the answers to the following test, using the space provided.

Essay Examination of Study Skills

Directions: Answer any two of the following questions.

1. *What suggestions could you make to a student who complains that he lacks the time to complete his assignments?*
2. *Briefly discuss the values of notetaking when reading.*

3. *Describe the construction and use of a master outline in preparing for an examination.*

(Make informal notes or an outline of your answers.)

Question No._____

_____

_____

_____

Question No. _____

_____

_____

_____

TASK 3: Budget your time.

Before you begin writing an essay exam, decide how much time you can afford to give to answering each question. (Have a watch with you so that you can carry out your budget plan.)

You might need up to ten minutes at the beginning of an exam for tasks 1, 2, and 3; allow five minutes at the end for proofreading your answers. Deduct these fifteen minutes from the total time to find out how much time you can spend answering questions. Then budget the time for your answers. Avoid allowing so much time for the first few questions that you cannot give proper treatment to the last questions.

Usually it is not wise to give equal time to all questions. Some questions can be answered quickly; others take time to think out carefully. You may want to jot down beside each question the amount of time you have budgeted for it.

Sometimes the directions will tell you that the questions are weighted differently. For example, the directions may say —

50 points will be given to question 1;
10 points each will be given to questions 2, 3, 4, 5, and 6.

You would spend considerably more time on question 1 than on any of the others, since it determines half your score.

Some questions take less time to answer than others. Consider the following two questions:

    (a) What were the names of Columbus's three ships?

    (b) Discuss Columbus's reaction to and relations with the American Indian.

As you can see, question *b* is more complex and will take longer than question *a*.

Show how much time you would allow to write each of the answers you outlined on the preceding page. Let us say the time limit for the exam is forty minutes. Remember to allow about ten minutes for tasks 1, 2, and 3. If you wish to save five minutes at the end for reading over your answers, you have twenty-five minutes in which to answer the questions.

Tasks 1, 2, 3	10 minutes
Proofreading	5 minutes
Question No. _____	_____ minutes
Question No. _____	_____ minutes

If you have budgeted unequal amounts of time for these questions, explain why.

_____

_____

_____

TASK 4: Begin a new paragraph for each point.

    With your outline before you, start writing your answers. You must write clearly and concisely. Good organization is particularly important. The simplest way to achieve this is to begin a new paragraph for each point. If a paragraph includes too many ideas, your instructor may think you have not bothered to think through the answers.

Practice this task by answering one of the questions you have just outlined. Keep to the time you have budgeted for it.

_____

_____

_____

_____

_____

_____

_____

_____

_____

_____

_____

_____

_____

_____

_____

_____

TASK 5:   Proofread your answers.

When you have finished the entire examination, read over what you have written in order to catch and correct careless statements. Try to allow five minutes for this as suggested under task 3. Be on the lookout for errors like these, where an example is given for each type.

Types of Errors

(a) Lack of clarity

> Einstein developed his photoelectric law, which became the basis of television in 1905.

(b) Misstatements

> Not until some time after the Civil War was King George willing to admit defeat.

(c) Vagueness

> In short, _Leaves of Grass_ is terrific poetry.

(d) Incorrect sentence structure

> Having solidified the gas, crystals were formed.

(e) Omitted words

> It illustrates certain which every student of health must bear in mind.

(f) Illegibility

(g) Punctuation errors

> Goethe said he had been learning to read for eighty years, however he was not satisfied with his progress.

(h) Misspelling

> In Professor Weaver's judgment, our dictionarys should contain a larger proportion of scientific terms than it does.

Correct the preceding examples of errors.

(a) _____

_____

(b) _____

_____

(c) _____

_____

(d) _____

_____

(e) _____

_____

(f) _____

_____

(g) _____

(h) _____

_____

TAKING OBJECTIVE EXAMINATIONS

TASK 1: Budget your time.

Look over the entire exam quickly to get some idea of its length. Note the number of sections and estimate how much time you should spend on each. Budget your time according to the relative difficulty of the questions. Also take into account the weighting of credit points per section. Then note the number of items in each section, and calculate roughly how much time you will have for each item. Allow a few minutes for budgeting, reading directions, proofreading.

If you were taking a two-part, sixty-minute exam, your time budget might look like the one shown here. (You will not, of course, have time to draw up a chart like this during an exam.)

You will need a watch to help you judge whether you are working at the right tempo as you go through the first few items. If you are not, adjust your speed accordingly.

History Exam — Time Limit: 60 Minutes

Activities	*Your Evaluation*	*Budgeted Time*	*Time for Each Item (Time ÷ Items)*
Budgeting time, reading directions	____	5 min.	____
Taking part I (50 true-false items)	easy	20 min.	24 sec.
Taking part II (50 multiple-choice items)	hard	30 min.	36 sec.
Proofreading answers	____	5 min.	____
Total time		60 min.	

TASK 2:   Underline important words in the directions.

The directions on an exam tell how to record the answers. Read them with care, so that you will not lose points for not following them. Again, as in an essay exam, underline important words in the directions to draw your attention to them.

Note how the following directions are underscored, and show how you would answer the item in accordance with the directions.
Write the <u>letter</u> of the correct answer <u>in front</u> of each statement.

_____ Australasia refers to (a) Australia and Asia (b) Australia and New Zealand (c) Australia

Examine the following statements of directions. In each statement underline the important words that tell you how to record your answer.

(a) In front of the number of each statement write a plus sign if it is true and a minus sign if it is false.

(b) Write the correct answer after each statement.

(c) With each item three completions are given. All are correct endings. Choose the best one of the three.

(d) Group A is a list of definitions. Group B is a list of terms. Decide which term is defined by each definition. Write the letter designating that term on the blank line before the definition.

TASK 3:   Consider hunches, but with caution.

What use can you make of impressions and vaguely remembered facts? That depends upon which of two methods of scoring will be used. Before the exam begins, find out from your instructor which of these two methods he will use:

(a) The score is determined by counting the number of correct answers. Guessing is not penalized.

(b) The score is determined by subtracting some number from the number of correct answers. Following are two common formulas used for determining this score.

Score = number of right answers − number of wrong answers

Score = number of right answers − $\frac{1}{4}$ number of wrong answers

Such formulas make it virtually impossible to get a good score by guessing. If method *b* is to be used, answer each item with extra caution. You will be safe in putting together an answer from related facts that you do recall.

Take the following exam item:

> The nation on the isthmus connecting Central America with South America is _____

Panama is the answer, but suppose you do not recall the location of all the individual Central American countries. You do know, however, the following facts:

> The Panama Canal cuts the isthmus.
>
> One Central American country is named Panama.

You reason that it is logical that the nation occupying the isthmus is Panama. You vaguely recall reading such a statement. Under these circumstances you would certainly be justified in writing *Panama* on the blank line.

It is also wise to try to eliminate all incorrect possibilities until one choice remains. That one may be the right answer. Suppose the following item appears in an exam:

> An example of a soft mineral is (a) quartz (b) talc (c) diamond

You may know nothing about talc, but you do know that quartz and diamond are hard minerals.

By eliminating the wrong choices, you therefore correctly conclude that the answer is talc.

One more hint about eliminating wrong answers: cross out the choices that are obviously incorrect. This will prevent your putting the wrong letter in the answer space in a hurried or flustered moment.

Of course you cannot successfully take an exam simply on hunches and your ability to eliminate wrong answers. But you can usually use facts and ideas you vaguely recollect on items you cannot answer immediately.

Try this method on the following items.

1. ____ In Buenos Aires, Argentina, spring begins on approximately the twenty-first day of (a) March (b) June (c) September

2. *Walden* was written by _____

3. T   F   The Union army was defeated at the Battle of Bull Run. (Circle T if true, F if false)

Disease	*Cause of disease*
4. ____ trichinosis	a. bacterium
5. ____ smallpox	b. virus
6. ____ tuberculosis	c. protozoan
	d. worm

Check the accuracy of your answers in an encyclopedia or other reference book. Which of the six items, if any, did you answer with certainty?

_____

Which items, if any, did you miss as a result of eliminating?

_____

Describe the hunches you followed.

_____

_____

_____

Which of the items, if any, did you answer correctly through elimination?

_____

Describe your reasoning in eliminating wrong answers.

_____

_____

Which items, if any, did you miss as a result of eliminating?

_____

How did your eliminating lead you astray?

_____

_____

TASK 4:   Underline important words in each item.

Sometimes in haste or because of overconfidence you may miss the significance of an important word in an item. Get into the habit of underlining significant words as you read. It will slow you down enough to make you read the items more carefully. Let us see how this works. Here is an objective exam question with suggested underlining:

The <u>Industrial</u> <u>Revolution</u> has contributed to <u>all</u> <u>but</u> <u>one</u> of the following (underline that one):

(a) A higher standard of living
(b) A movement to rural areas
(c) More rapid communication
(d) Imperialism

Note the importance of the phrase <u>all</u> <u>but</u> <u>one</u>.

Underline important words in the following items:

1. The United States and French governments have always been on friendly terms.

2. Transistors can be used to replace (a) fuses (b) electron tubes (c) switches (d) condensers

3. A Norwegian musician who was a contemporary of the Norwegian dramatist Ibsen is (a) Hamsun (b) Undset (c) Grieg (d) Bjornson

4. A monthly periodical devoted almost exclusively to keeping the businessman informed of events and trends is (a) *Time* (b) *Fortune* (c) *Newsweek* (d) *Nation*

Also be on the lookout for closed words like *never, only,* and *always* in true-false questions. Underline them. Items with such words are generally false, especially in the social sciences.

These are typical items with closed words, and they are both wrong. Underscore the closed word or words in each.

5. The United States and French governments have always been on friendly terms.

6. Prices never go down when demand decreases.

Underscore closed words in this multiple-choice item:

7. Organisms capable of spontaneous movement are (a) always animals (b) primarily animals (c) never plants (d) occasionally animals

On the other hand, closed words in some items, such as those defining certain scientific concepts, may express a true statement. For example:

All bases can neutralize acids to form a salt.

Using a closed word, make up a true-false item that is untrue.

Now make it into a true statement by substituting for the closed word one of the open words such as usually, frequently, mostly, sometimes.

TASK 5:   Answer the easy items first.

In an objective exam you have two goals: (1) to answer as many questions as you can and (2) to answer them correctly. In all objective exams the more right answers you have the better your score will be. Go through the exam quickly, marking the items where you are sure of the answers. Mark the more difficult items in the margin for easy spotting when you return to them.

In an objective exam all items usually have the same value, so there is no point in wasting time on troublesome ones. If the test is long, you may lose some points by not completing the exam. This task will help you achieve the highest possible score by enabling you to finish as much as you can within the time limits.

Another reason for tackling the easy items first is that they may provide leads for answering more difficult ones.

Let us suppose you do not know the answer to this item:

The basic component of coal is _____

You skip over it, going on to answer only the items you are sure of, until you have completed the entire test. One of the later items reads:

The chief element of graphite, coal, and charcoal is (a) plutonium (b) tungsten (c) carbon (d) silicon

This brings to mind the fact that carbon is the basic element of coal. When you go over the exam a second time to answer the harder items, you write *carbon* in the space where it belongs. Had you stopped to ponder it, you would have wasted a lot of time and perhaps not have come up with the answer.

TASK 6:   Interpret items with common sense.

The more you labor over an objective item, the more likely you are to read something into it that your instructor did not intend. Look at this item:

Three documents that are landmarks in the progress of human liberty are dated 1215, 1776, and 1789. The document having the most to do with American institutions is dated (a) 1215 (b) 1776 (c) 1789.

You are not sure which date is the right one. Let us say that you do know that the documents referred to are the Magna Charta, the Declaration of

Independence, and the Declaration of the Rights of Man. Common sense tells you that *b* is the answer. You think further about it, however, and reason that the Declaration of Independence was drawn from the Magna Charta. Maybe your answer should be *a*. Such reasoning is risky. It is much more likely that your first idea — the more obvious answer — is the correct one.

TASK 7:   Proofread your answers.

Try to finish the exam five minutes before the time is up in order to look over your answers briefly, as planned in your time budget. Here is a suggested procedure for proofreading:

1. Reread the items and questions to make sure you answered them correctly and completely. For example, one question in a science exam reads: What are the purposes of a chimney? Four choices were given for answers: (a) furnishes a draft; (b) enhances the architecture; (c) carries off smoke and gases; (d) reduces fuel consumption. Upon proofreading, you notice the word purposes (plural) in the question. You had checked only *a* for your answer. When you look over the answers again, you realize that *c* is also a basic purpose for a chimney; so now you check it also.

2. Make sure you put down the answer you intended on each item. It is annoying to learn that you failed a question because you carelessly wrote down the wrong letter or marked the wrong item. Suppose you know the correct answer to the following item.

> True   False   Rotation of crops restores nitrogen to the soil.

You know this is true. Yet, in haste or carelessness or both, you underline <u>False</u>. In proofreading, you will usually catch such an item and correct it, thereby salvaging a few points for yourself.

3. Go over some of the more troublesome items. If you have marked these in the margin, you can easily spot them. For example, suppose you are unsure of the answer to this question:

> _____ Franklin D. Roosevelt first appeared on a presidential ticket in (a) 1920 (b) 1932 (c) 1936 (d) 1940.

Returning to it in the last five minutes might give you time to recall that he ran for vice-president in 1920. So you correctly put *a* on the blank line.

4. Make sure every answer you have written or marked is legible and clear.

Now try out all seven of the tasks in "Taking Objective Examinations" on the following practice exam.

Practice Exam

Directions: *You will have ten minutes to take the exam. The score will be the number of correct answers. Apply all the "tasks" in working on the exam.*

True-false items: *On the line before each statement, write T for true or F for false.*

1. _____ The British constitution is a single written document similar to the U.S. Constitution.

2. _____ Rheumatic fever always follows a streptococcal infection.

3. _____ Heat is a form of energy.

Multiple-choice items: *Write the letter of the correct completion in front of each statement.*

4. _____ The plateau in the center of Athens is called
   a. the Parthenon   c. Mount Olympus
   b. the Acropolis   d. Sparta

5. _____ A sudden and complete change in government as a result of force is called a
   a. blitzkrieg   c. coup d'état
   b. revolution   d. plebiscite

6. _____ The sewing machine was invented in 1846 by
   a. Howe   c. Edison
   b. McCormick   d. Fulton

Matching items: *Group A is a list of definitions. Group B is a list of fields of study. Decide which field of study is defined by each of the definitions and write the appropriate letter on the blank line.*

Group A   *Group B*

7. _____ Study of behavior   a. Paleontology

8. _____ Study of material remains of past human life   b. Anthropology

   c. Psychology

9. _____ Study of man   d. Archaeology

Completion items: *Complete each statement by writing one word on the blank line.*

10. The ruler of ancient Egypt was called a _____

11. Desert people who are perpetual wanderers are called _____

12. The belief that there is only one God is called _____

In taking the exam, did you —	(Circle Y for Yes or N for No)	
budget your time?	Y	N
underline important words in the directions?	Y	N
consider hunches with caution?	Y	N
underline important words in each item?	Y	N
answer the easy items first?	Y	N
interpret items with common sense?	Y	N
proofread your answers?	Y	N

Check your answers to the practice exam, against this key:

1. F	5. c	9. b
2. F	6. a	10. Pharaoh
3. T	7. c	11. nomads
4. b	8. d	12. monotheism

EXTRA PRACTICE

Take the examination on *"Psychology,"* which begins on page 169, and on *"Vitamins,"* which begins on page 171. Apply the procedures described in this chapter.

A Bird's-Eye View of Taking Examinations

Essay Exams

1. Underline important words in the directions.
2. Outline your answers.
3. Budget your time.
4. Begin a new paragraph for each point.
5. Proofread your answers.

Objective Exams

1. Budget your time.
2. Underline important words in the directions.
3. Consider hunches, but with caution.
4. Underline important words in each item.
5. Answer the easy items first.
6. Interpret items with common sense.
7. Proofread your answers.

How to Broaden Your Reading Base

Are you a textbook-only reader?

In chapters 2–5 of this book you learned a definite strategy for mastering textbook assignments. But reading about a subject in a textbook, only, is far from adequate if you want to be really at home with the subject. A textbook is, after all, a formal treatment of selected topics by an author or authors who usually "boil down" those topics. The restricted space in a textbook means that the treatment of the topics must be confined to the highlights of the ideas discussed. Few topics are presented in depth in a textbook.

If you want to overcome the limitations of textbook-only reading and broaden your reading base, you should plan to do some outside reading and do it critically and with appropriate speed.

TASK 1: Read broadly and deeply.

Students sometimes testify to the importance to them of reading broadly and deeply. One student reported that it was the outside reading in a course he took in history that kept it from being the "driest and dullest" of all courses. Another student said that historical novels supplied the human touch that she found lacking in her history textbook, and they often raised her curiosity about details that she satisfied by still further reading. A student taking a chemistry course told us it was interesting and valuable for her to browse through science magazines and journals in the library and to discover practical applications and controversies relating to principles being learned in class. These students clearly believe that extended reading both enlivens their interest and enriches their understanding of the subject being studied.

Suppose you are studying immunity against disease in a biology course and would like to know more about the pioneer work of Jenner and Pasteur. Your textbook tells just enough to make you aware that this is a fascinating subject. You may want to read freely to satisfy your curiosity and not bother with notes. On the other hand, you may wish to take the kind of notes described in chapter 3.

(1) First, you might consult the card catalog in the library. The cards in this catalog cover every book in the library and are arranged alphabetically. You can look up a book by searching for its title, the author's name, or the subject.

You look in the card catalog under the headings "Jenner," "Pasteur," and "Immunity." You may find ten book titles in the catalog. But suppose only two of them have titles that make you think they will supply the information you are interested in.

Using index cards, you copy from the catalog's cards the information necessary to locate these two books.

(2) You could also browse in the stacks. The stacks are compactly arranged bookcases containing the major part of the library's collection of books. The books in the stacks are arranged according to call number. You find out from the card catalog (or the librarian) what letters or numbers are used to mark the books on immunity and biography and where the books are located. In browsing, you may discover that certain books that you had rejected or ignored when looking at their cards in the card catalog provide you with interesting information after all. One of the older books, for example, might have some excellent pictures of the laboratory apparatus used by Pasteur.

(3) You could consult the *Readers' Guide to Periodical Literature*. Ask the librarian where to find it. It is published semimonthly and is cumulatively bound each year. Articles that appear in selected periodicals of general interest are included in these reference books. If you want recent articles on Jenner or Pasteur, you look for the latest edition of the *Readers' Guide*. You can work back into earlier editions if necessary until you find something about one or both of these scientists. You copy the information about each likely article listed in the *Readers' Guide*. The librarian can direct you to guides that list more technical articles than does the *Readers' Guide*. Scholarly articles on immunity, for example, are indexed in *Biological Abstracts*.

(4) You could consult an encyclopedia. Before you finish your browsing, you may want to glance at an expert's summary of your subject — which is what an encyclopedia's article is. This can serve as a check on the completeness of your browsing.

Choose any topic you are now studying in one of your courses. Go to the library and examine books and articles on the subject. Answer the following questions.

What topic have you chosen? _____

How many references on this topic do you find in the card catalog? _____

Judging by the titles and dates, how many of these look helpful? _____

Give the following information concerning any one of the more helpful-looking references:

   Call number _____ *Date of publication or copyright* _____

   Author (in full) _____

   Title _____

How many of these helpful-looking books are you able to locate in the library?

_____

In your visit to the stacks, how many helpful books do you find? (Omit those you made notes on when you examined the card catalog.)

_____

Give information about one of them:

   Call number _____ *Date of publication or copyright* _____

   Author (in full) _____

   Title _____

What encyclopedia did you use? _____

What important phases of your topic omitted in your browsing are discussed in the encyclopedia?

_____

TASK 2:   Read critically.

When you read critically, you interpret and judge the author's statements. You try to link facts and conclusions. You judge whether the author implies more than he or she actually states. You must be able to evaluate, if you are to really understand a book or article. Here are some suggestions for learning to read critically:

(1) Try to determine the intent of the author. Is the author writing a simple, literal, objective report? Or giving imagination free play? Or attempting to explain something? Or trying to persuade you of the value of something? Of course the author could intend to do all of these in different places in the book or article.

(2) In reading difficult textbooks and reference books, analyze every paragraph to discover its purpose. One of the following is usually true of a given paragraph:

   (a) The paragraph tells about cause-and-effect relationships (such as factors contributing to a city's growth).
   (b) The paragraph gives an objective account of a process (such as how to produce oxygen in the laboratory).
   (c) The paragraph makes comparisons or draws contrasts (such as descriptions of Pueblo culture and contemporary urban culture in America).
   (d) The paragraph lists something (such as the causes of the Vietnam War).
   (e) The paragraph tells something chronologically (such as the steps in the manufacture of paper).

(3) Separate statements of fact from statements of opinion. Even authors of straightforward, objective textbooks express occasional opinions. This may be entirely justifiable and helpful. An authority on economics, for example, after presenting in a book the conflicting and confusing views of others on the cure for inflation, may decide to weigh the facts and offer his or her own conclusions. A critical reader is aware when an author is doing this.

(4) If the writing is full of startling or unlikely statements, seek information from *Who's Who* or some other source concerning the author's qualifications.

(5) If you suspect the author is subtly (or with a snow job!) trying to persuade you to a certain way of thinking, put up your guard! Weigh the arguments with care.

(6) Spot words, phrases, and sentences that authors use deliberately to arouse such emotions as anger, fear, or bitterness, which interfere with the exercise of rational judgment.

You need to explore such questions in connection with some of your extended reading if you are to exercise your ability to make wise judgments as you read.

Now take some current issue and read several sources so that you can evaluate each in terms of the six suggestions given above. Indicate on the next page the issue or problem you want to explore.

Issue _____

Source 1. _____

Source 2. _____

Source 3. _____

Source 4. _____

What conclusions have you reached as a result of your reading of these several sources?

_____

_____

_____

TASK 3:   Read at appropriate speeds.

There is no correct rate of reading for everyone. Some people are able to read faster than others. The comfortable speed at which some can recognize and understand printed words is faster than that of other people. People differ in reading speed just as they do in the speed with which they can run or wash the car or get dressed.

Good readers do not read everything at the same rate; they are flexible. They read rapidly when it suits their purposes and needs. They slow up when they have to in order to understand, enjoy, or reflect upon the content. Clifton Fadiman commented wisely on the importance of reading flexibility, noting that worthwhile material might be read with tortoise deliberation while trash should be read with the speed of light.

You have already learned the mastery technique for reading your textbooks more efficiently. Clearly, there was no emphasis on speed as such. Using the mastery technique, you will require less time in the long run to learn an assignment than if you read and reread the material without a knowledge of the steps and procedures of efficient study.

You will read difficult material that contains new terms, technical information, and concepts at a slower rate than you would read narrative material. You will need to stop often to figure out word meanings, to try to form a mental image, or to take in a new idea.

Try reading the following passage rapidly:

When botanists breed a tall strain of pea, all the plants of the second generation are tall. When they breed the plants of the second generation,

75 percent of the third generation are tall and 25 percent are short. Tallness in this case is called dominant and shortness is called recessive.

You are apt to slow down and even reread a passage like this, especially if you are studying genetics for the first time. The reasons for slowing down are fairly obvious: (1) A complicated law of genetics is packed into a few sentences. (2) Two technical terms are introduced (*dominant, recessive*). (3) The meaning of the words is given in mathematical terms. (4) An intricate relationship is suggested (the proportion of tall and short plants is a function of generation).

You cannot expect to speed through technical material as you might through a popular novel.

You should use another speed when you read some well-written novels and poetry. They often express interesting and beautiful thoughts in unique ways. You may want to savor them, to pause to digest a new idea here or to enjoy the writer's style there.

Consider this bit of poetry:

> A primrose by a river's brim
> A yellow primrose was to him,
> And it was nothing more.

You might want to take a moment to admire this skillful summing up of callous, uninspired Peter Bell in these lines by Wordsworth.

Both technical material and artistic writing will slow you down, but do not let that discourage you from learning to read articles, stories, newspapers, and similar material much faster.

You can greatly increase your rate of this kind of reading by practicing the following rules: (1) select easy material; (2) preview; (3) time yourself and force yourself to read more rapidly; (4) recite from time to time.

(1) Practice on easy, interesting reading matter. The quickest road to the knack of faster reading is practice on material that is easy for you. To read rapidly, your eyes must develop the habit of moving swiftly and your mind the habit of uninterrupted reading. The best way to acquire these habits is to begin with stories and articles that do not contain too many unfamiliar words and ideas. It is well also to begin with a subject or story that sounds particularly interesting. It is always easier to read interesting material than something that bores you.

(2) Preview the material. As you learned in the mastery technique, previewing is a search for structure—for the main outline. All reading material has structure. As we have seen, textbooks typically point up this structure rather elaborately through headings, italics, and the like. The lighter narrative material we are concerned with here does not use these signals very often. A rapid survey of the material, however—looking for introductory and concluding paragraphs, for topic sentences, and for

names of persons involved in the story—is helpful in getting the whole picture. (In the case of fiction where you do not want to spoil the story by reading ahead, you should ignore this step.)

(3) Time yourself and force yourself to read more rapidly. Using some periodical like *Reader's Digest* or an easy novel you have wanted to read, find out how many pages you can read in fifteen minutes at your usual rate.

Develop a visual record on the graph below, which now shows five pages read in fifteen minutes on a first reading.

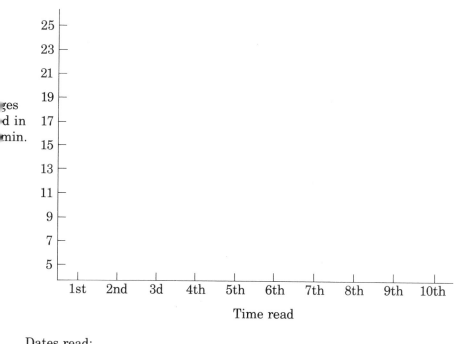

Dates read:

Sept. 10 _____ _____ _____

_____ _____ _____ _____

_____ _____ _____ _____

On successive trials, record your progress on the graph by showing the number of pages you read in the same amount of time. Before each fifteen-minute speed run, you should practice on similar material for at least an hour, forcing yourself to read more rapidly. Just the intention to read more rapidly will usually improve your speed. In addition, you should force yourself to read faster than is comfortable by using a pacing technique such as moving your hand or a 3×5 card down the page, line by line. At first you may find you are self-conscious and that your attention is only on part of your reading. After a few pages, however, you will adjust to this advanced speed and will again concentrate on the subject.

(4) Recite to yourself from time to time as explained in chapter 3 in order to check on your comprehension. There is obviously no point in gaining speed at the expense of understanding.

A deliberate program of self-improvement like the one described can improve your speed on material you read by 50 to 100 percent or more.

EXTRA PRACTICE

Practice the four rules stated in Task 3 for increasing reading speed, using any three selections in the "Practice Materials" section at the end of this book.

A Bird's-Eye View of Broadening Your Reading Base

1. Read broadly and deeply.
2. Read critically.
3. Read at appropriate speeds.

10

How to Write a Report

Next to reading, writing is your most important tool for school and college work. In practically every subject you have to write at some time. Your instructors will judge your ability, to a very large degree, by the quality of your writing in reports, term papers, book reviews, summaries, and compositions of all kinds.

Throughout life you will probably write many letters, messages, and reports. A part of your success both in and out of school may be determined by your ability to write clearly and to the point. If you write well, people who read your writing will know exactly what you are trying to say. You will not be misunderstood. Your writing will gain respect for you and for the points you have brought out.

TASK 1: Collect and organize information and ideas on your subject.

Once you have chosen your subject, but before you write a single paragraph, collect all the information and ideas you will need. Take a stack of 3 × 5 cards. Jot down topics you know you will want to discuss, using a separate card for each topic. Also jot down any good idea as it comes to you, one to a card. As you note these topics and ideas, your mind begins to work them over. Soon you will get an idea of how you want to handle your subject and what information you will have to track down.

Take the cards with you to the library and start reading – searching for that needed information. As explained in the previous chapter, the card catalog will show you what books the library has on the subject. The *Readers' Guide to Periodical Literature* will lead you to many magazine articles on the subject. Don't neglect the scholarly indexes (*Biological Abstracts, Psychological Abstracts, Social Sciences and Humanities*, and others).

Your next step is to sort the cards in piles representing what you think would make suitable sections of your report. You also can begin arranging these piles in a row to show the order in which you plan to write each section. This is another way in which your stack of cards helps you organize your paper.

While you "play solitaire" in this way, you may discover that some of the ideas jotted on the cards really aren't needed. So cross them out. You may also find that some cards deal with a phase of your subject that now doesn't fit in well with your report as it is beginning to shape up. Discard those cards. And, finally, as you look over your cards, you may become aware that you have failed to deal with some important phase of the subject that ought to be taken up. Make out new cards with the new ideas on them. Do it at once, before you forget. As soon as you have a chance, do some more reading in the library with these cards before you.

Select a topic on which you intend to report.

Topic _____

Prepare a set of 3 × 5 cards. Sort them into piles, each of which contains related information.

Arrange these card piles in the order in which you plan to use them in your report. List the topics below in that order.

1. _____

2. _____

3. _____

4. _____

5. _____

6. _____

Give the topics of any cards that you decide not to use.

_____

_____

What topic, information, or idea, if any, for which you do not now have a card, should be included? Topic of card:

_____

_____

TASK 2:   Make an outline.

The outline is the next step in organizing your thoughts. Making an outline forces you to be logical. It helps you to see more clearly the relation between major points and minor points and makes it easier for you to decide how to arrange them. When you write your paper, the outline keeps your thinking on the beam.

An outline has been standardized for convenience. If you follow the standard plan for your outlines, you can hand them to any educated person — your instructor, for instance — for discussion or criticism and he or she will be able to understand your plan at a glance.

A report, "Water Transportation in the United States," was organized into the following six major sections: early river transportation, canals, river steamboats, inland waterway system, coastwise and intercoastal shipping, and future of water transportation. An outline that was drawn up in preparation for writing the report begins like this:

Water Transportation in the United States
I.   Early river transportation
    A. Early settlements dependent on water transportation
        1. Roads in poor condition
        2. Downstream river transportation convenient and economical
            (a) Rafts, flatboats, etc., inexpensive to build and operate
            (b) Numerous navigable rivers along seaboard
    B. Inadequacies of river transportation
        1. Slow
        2. Rivers subject to freezing in winter
        3. Upstream traffic difficult and expensive
            (a) Flatboats often sold for lumber after downstream run
            (b) Rivers' falls necessitate portaging

II. Canals
    A. Canal building competed with road improvement
        1. Canal transportation had advantage over roads: greater economy; power supplied by horses and mules (pulled barges with ropes)
        2. First canals: channels to bypass falls
            (a) Examples: on Merrimack and Connecticut rivers
            (b) Federal aid often supplied
            (c) Mostly privately owned and profitable
    B. Transmountain canals
        1. Examples: Erie Canal and Pennsylvania Public Works
        2. Connected seaboard navigation with Ohio River and Great Lakes

This portion of one outline may give you an idea of the form of outlining and its value as a writing guide. The writer has only to follow it point by point in writing his report. Main points (I, II), subpoints (A, B), and sub-subpoints (1, 2, 3) stand out clearly in order of their rank.

Take the topic you selected on page 124 and, using the cards you prepared, make an outline of it.

Your Example of an Outline

TASK 3:   Organize each paragraph.

Now that you have made an outline, you are ready to begin writing. Paragraph organization is the key to good writing. Usually the first word of a paragraph is indented to set it off from other paragraphs. Open any book and notice how you can count the paragraphs on a page in less than a second. The eye easily notes the paragraphs. The paragraphs should be set off from each other not only by their arrangement but also by their content. Each paragraph should have a topic, and, conversely, for every major topic you will need a new paragraph. Sometimes even a subpoint in an outline deserves a separate paragraph.

On the other hand, you might wish to combine several subpoints in one paragraph if you don't have much to write about each one, and want to show their close relationship. Remember, the outline is just to help you clear your thinking and decide the order of topics.

Look at your outline on page 126. Give an example of a subtopic that might deserve a separate paragraph.

_____

_____

For the sake of clarity, get in the habit of trying to express the topic of each paragraph in a single sentence before starting to write the paragraph. This is a check on whether the paragraph really has a topic. Perhaps it is a jumble of topics. If you can't express the topic in a sentence, you can be sure something is wrong and the paragraph won't be a good one.

Think about the first paragraph for the report you have outlined. In one sentence, what is it about?

_____

_____

You have just written a topic sentence.

The first sentence of the following paragraph is also a topic sentence:

The metric system has several advantages over the system of weights and measures commonly used in the United States. It establishes a uniform relationship within any given category of measurement—for example, distance. Because the metric system is a decimal system, one can convert from one unit to a unit of different size simply by moving the decimal point. Moreover, since the standards of measuring area and volume are derived from the standard of length, linear measurement, capacity, and weight are interrelated. The metric system is widely used throughout the world.

Make a practice of composing a topic sentence for each paragraph, and generally use it as the first sentence of the paragraph. But don't be rigid about its location; sometimes it can be placed more appropriately elsewhere in the paragraph. The topic sentence will help the readers grasp your explanation, criticism, description, praise, proof, argument, or whatever it is you are writing. They will know quickly what you propose to talk about. They can then deal with the details of the paragraph, knowing exactly what you are explaining.

Sometimes the first sentence should show that the new paragraph is related to the one just completed. Following are examples of this:

But if the heart seems to be a busy organ, consider the liver.

Another reason for learning a musical instrument in childhood is the ease with which the child responds automatically.

In doing this—using a transitional sentence—you mention the topic in the preceding paragraph as well as the topic of the present one. Such transitions carry the reader smoothly from one thought to the next.

Give another example, either from a book or of your own invention.

_____

_____

_____

One final suggestion concerning the composition of the paragraph: Be sure to include all the material that belongs there. Don't scatter its parts in other paragraphs where they do not belong. A well-constructed outline will prevent your jumping around and will keep you in line.

On this and the next page, write a brief report for which you have already made an outline (page 126).

Example of Report

Topic _____

Example of Report (continued)

Check your written report against these four points:

	Yes	No
Every important topic has a paragraph.		
Every paragraph has a topic sentence.		
Each paragraph contains what belongs there.		
Each paragraph contains only what belongs there.		

If you have found it necessary to place a check for any of the above items in the "no" column, go over your report and correct the situation.

TASK 4:   Make each sentence clear.

Clear understanding depends on clear writing. Clear writing depends on clear sentences. Here are some rules to guide you in making each sentence clear:

1. Express a complete idea in every sentence.

The commonest errors are made in sentences containing clauses. Certain clauses (called subordinate clauses) cannot stand alone because they do not express complete ideas. For example:

(a) By the end of March 1909
(b) Before the nitric acid is added
(c) Although many narcotics are habit-forming
(d) Much as Churchill regretted the delay

Clauses like these are tricky because they generally contain a subject and a predicate. For that reason, some students think they are sentences.

Make each of the above clauses into a complete sentence. The first one has been completed as an example.

(a) By the end of March 1909 Peary had made his last main camp.

(b) _____

_____

(c) _____

_____

(d) _____

_____

Sometimes incomplete sentences are acceptable for literary effect. For example:

> Hurstwood, one of Dreiser's most memorable characters, was stripped of his wealth. To the very last dollar.

> The queen declared she would never see the ambassador again. Not ever again.

Give an example of an acceptable incomplete sentence that follows a complete sentence.

_____

_____

_____

_____

Avoid writing more than an occasional incomplete sentence. Few reports assigned by your instructors would make such sentences appropriate. For the most part, clarity requires a flow of sentences expressing a logical flow of thought, with each sentence stating a complete idea.

2. Control the length of your sentences. In general, keep them brief but not choppy, and do not have them so long that they are hard to follow.

Compare the three paragraphs in the first column; then compare those in the second column.

Long, Stringy Sentences

Swinton proclaimed his innocence in the holdup, yet he did not deny that he had chosen weak companions, nor did he deny that he had a lust for money; but he insisted that he had even taken the trouble to report what he knew to the police.

Although the geographic North Pole, at which the meridians meet, indicates the direction of true north, there is also a second north position, called the Magnetic North Pole, to which magnetic compasses point.

Short, Choppy Sentences

Swinton proclaimed his innocence. He admitted choosing weak companions. He admitted a lust for money. But he said he acted honorably. He said he reported what he knew. He reported it to the police.

There are two north poles. One is the geographic North Pole. It indicates the direction of true north. The meridians meet there. Then there is the second north pole position. It is called the Magnetic North Pole. Magnetic compasses point to it.

Sentences of Normal Length

Swinton proclaimed his innocence in the holdup. He did not deny that he had chosen weak companions or that he had a lust for money. He insisted, however, that he had acted honorably. Furthermore, he stated he had even taken the trouble to report what he knew to the police.

The geographic North Pole, at which the meridians meet, indicates the direction of true north. There is, however, another north position. That is the Magnetic North Pole, to which magnetic compasses point.

You can readily see how much more smoothly and easily the third set of paragraphs reads and how much clearer the paragraphs are. Sentences of moderate brevity as a rule make the reading seem more interesting also.

Give an example of a sentence of normal length.

_____

_____

There are some ideas, however, that make a long sentence necessary. Definitions and scientific principles are often stated in long sentences to show their related ideas. Here are examples:

Photosynthesis is the formation of carbohydrates in the chlorophyll-containing tissues of plants by a process in which chloroplasts combine water and carbon dioxide of the air with the aid of radiant energy, especially light.

The Furies were three goddesses of Greek mythology whose heads were wreathed with serpents and who punished, by secretly stinging them, humans who had escaped any deserved punishment from their fellow humans.

Give an example of your own of a long sentence that is permissible.

_____

_____

_____

Choppy sentences have their place too, particularly when you wish to show snappy action or suspense. But few assignments call for this kind of writing.

3. See that nothing in your sentences is left dangling.

Look at this sentence:

Working all night, the assignment was completed.

You will note that "working all night" is not related to the remainder of the sentence. The sentence could be correctly rewritten as follows:

Working all night, the student completed the assignment.

Underline the dangling parts of the following sentences and then rewrite the sentences.

Having solidified the gas, crystals were formed.

_____

_____

Being a shallow brook, the fish were few.

_____

_____

Reaching Bunker Hill, the monument was evident.

_____

_____

4. Construct each sentence so that it has only one meaning.

You can accomplish this by making it obvious to which part of the sentence your words and phrases refer. Study the following sentence:

> The sales manager agreed each week to write to her sales agents.

The reader cannot tell whether the sales manager *agreed* each week or agreed to *write* each week. The sentence could be straightened out as follows:

> The sales manager agreed to write to her sales agents each week.

Rewrite each of the following unclear sentences.

Napoleon ordered his men slowly to retreat.

_____

_____

The social worker handed a list of cases of extreme hardship to the mayor.

_____

_____

Professor Dodd wrote to Einstein about how he solved the problem at once.

_____

_____

The Harts wished to adopt one more child from an orphanage under three years old.

_____

_____

TASK 5: Use words accurately.

Each word has its own meaning or meanings and its own proper use or uses. The correct use of words determines to a large extent how clear your writing will be. Two words that do not have the same meaning element cannot be used interchangeably (for example, *respectfully* and *respectively*). If you have trouble deciding what word to use in any situation, consult a dictionary. Here are examples of some common errors in word usage:

On this matter Madison believed *different* (instead of *differently*) after he became president.

A relatively small *percent* (instead of *percentage*) of the national income is paid in the form of profits.

Today's decision by the Supreme Court is of *transcendental* (instead of *transcendent*) importance.

The following words, arranged in pairs, are sometimes confused. Consult your dictionary if necessary, and write a sentence for each of the following words that will show that you know its correct meaning.

invent _____

discover _____

custom _____

habit _____

later _____

latter _____

imply _____

infer _____

affect _____

effect _____

disinterested _____

uninterested _____

defective _____

deficient _____

In the following sentences, cross out the word or words used incorrectly and write the corrected word or words in the space provided.

Congress adapted the resolution with only a few dissenting votes.

_____

The contents of the test tube weighed 28 grams, e.g., about one ounce.

_____

Throughout this trying period, Dickens never left go of his ambition to write a mystery.

_____

Robert Owen was an idealist and sought to establish an earthy paradise.

_____

A state commission censures all films before they are shown publicly.

_____

TASK 6: Supply enough detail to make your writing definite.

To write effectively, you must give your reader a clear-cut idea of what you are trying to say. A good practice is to go back over your writing after it is finished, supplying detailed examples where they will inform the reader and cutting out threadbare clichés, which tend to make any writing dull.

Here is a paragraph from a first draft of a student's report:

> The Incas, those denizens of the forest, provided education for the few. Only members of the nobility could attend the Yachahuasi, and it goes without saying, only the male members at that. The poor but honest nobodies never had a chance. Here the nobility learned the tools and traditions of the Incas and warfare in all its phases. A stiff examination followed graduation; but that's another story.

This paragraph is intended to describe briefly the educational system of the Incas of Peru. Do you consider it a clear description? Does it explain the facts—what the Yachahuasi is, or what tools and traditions were learned? If you did not know these things, you would not learn them from reading this paragraph.

The student could improve the report as follows: Cross out the tiresome expressions that say nothing. Substitute explanatory phrases that will give the reader a more definite picture of the Incas and their educational system. Eliminate trite and useless phrases. Here are a few specific examples.

Cross Out	Substitute
those denizens of the forest	Indians of Peru who created an efficient, prosperous civilization often compared to that of the Roman Empire
and it goes without saying, only the male members at that	a sort of national college for boys between twelve and sixteen
but that's another story	it included tests of their athletic ability as boxers, wrestlers, and runners and their ability to survive fasting and mock combat with dulled weapons

Eliminate	Supply Examples
The poor but honest nobodies never had a chance.	Here the nobility learned the tools
in all its phases	especially the use of the knot record (a primitive writing system) and weapons of war. They learned the Inca traditions contained in their religion, folklore, social organization, and customs.

The paragraph now reads:

> Another example of education for the few is found in the educational system of the Incas, Indians of Peru who created an efficient, prosperous civilization often compared to that of the Roman Empire. Only members of the nobility could attend the Yachahuasi, a sort of national college for boys between twelve and sixteen. Here the nobility learned the Inca tools, especially the use of the knot record (a primitive writing system) and weapons of war. They learned the Inca traditions contained in their religion, folklore, social organization, and customs. A stiff examination followed their graduation; it included tests of their athletic ability as boxers, wrestlers, and runners and their ability to survive fasting and mock combat with dulled weapons.

You can readily see how much more detailed, clear, and vivid this revised paragraph is than the original. Yet it is not much longer. Here is another example of foggy writing:

> In early childhood, Benjamin Franklin was recognized as a budding genius.

Budding genius is a tiresome cliché that lacks clarity. Something like this would be an improvement:

> In his early childhood Benjamin Franklin showed ability. He learned to read long before entering school. In his first year at school he rose rapidly from the middle to the head of his class.

Rewrite the following sentences, making your writing vivid by using concrete detail:

Bolivar deeply resented the centuries during which Venezuela and other South American countries had been misruled by Spain, and eventually blew his top.

_____

_____

After his marriage, John Bunyan, the mischief-loving youth, learned to walk the straight and narrow.

_____

_____

He believes intelligence tests are terrible.

_____

_____

After a good night's rest, Washington felt as fresh as a daisy.

_____

_____

The paintings of Andrew Wyeth are wonderful.

_____

_____

TASK 7:   Rewrite your first drafts.

Task 6 demonstrates why you need to develop the habit of reading over what you write and making changes for the better. You should definitely plan to rewrite your first draft of every written assignment. Most professional writers make it a regular practice to go over their material and take it for granted they will have to rewrite it—sometimes several times. Rewriting will enhance your understanding and recall of the subjects and will result in smoother writing and hence more pleasurable reading. It will also result in a better mark than would a carelessly written paper.

Read aloud what you have written. You can tell better by oral than by silent reading if any of your phrases or sentences sound crude, clumsy, unconvincing, too long, too stuffy, or too sentimental. Look at the following sentence:

> Grover Cleveland was fat.

Do you think the word *fat* sounds well as used here? Actually its use is crude, and you would not find it in careful writing. *Stout* or *on the portly side* would be better.

This is from a biology report on spiders:

> The silk of the spider's web comes from small appendages at the end of the abdomen. They discharge a fluid that hardens when exposed to the air. It is a delicate, fairylike lace.

On rereading, you may conclude that the last sentence is too lyrical for a scientific report, so you delete it.

Suppose you had written this:

> The President addressed Congress. His message was succinct and brief.

On rereading, you would probably see that *brief* adds nothing to succinct and would cross out *and brief.*
Or take this sentence:

> Better that every glimmering star should turn to darkness than that we should eliminate the protective tariff.

How would you rewrite it to eliminate its bombast?

_____

_____

_____

Below and on the next pages rewrite the report that you drafted on pages 129 and 130 of this chapter.

Rewritten Report

Topic _____

Rewritten Report (continued)

Rewritten Report (continued)

TASK 8: Learn to spell accurately.

One of the common criticisms of American schools is that their students cannot spell. This is too sweeping a criticism, but it is true that many students do not spell well.

Is sound-spelling dependable?   Have you been bothered because many English words are not spelled as they sound? American students of Spanish and German often find spelling in those languages easier than in English. Why? Because in those languages both the vowel and consonant sounds are more consistently represented by the letters with those sounds. If in English each sound were always represented by the same letter or group of letters, we could spell any word once we learned the sound-letter relationships.

One example of the dilemma we face in the English language is the sound of *sh* as in *shall*. This sound is also heard in the following words, but is spelled differently in each: *station, sure, special, Chicago, mission.*

Spelling in English cannot be approached on the same basis as in languages in which the phonetic sounds of letters and spelling are more consistently related. The study of sounds becomes one aid, but if we depended on sound alone, we would misspell the above words: *stashun, shure, speshul, Shikago, mishon.*

What words should be learned?   There are more than 200,000 words in a good dictionary. Must you learn the spelling of all of these? No. Studies have shown that 1 percent of these words—just 2000—make up approximately 90 to 95 percent of the vocabulary used by the typical person in writing. These words are available in spelling books from practically any publisher. They should be mastered by every student. Approximately 10 percent of them are troublemakers. These words are worth your serious attention.

Since you are well beyond grade 8, you may wonder why the performance of eighth-graders is given. There are no statistics on the performance of older students in spelling these words. It is true that college freshmen spell better than eighth-grade students, but not spectacularly so. On one eighth-grade test, students completing high school misspelled 20 percent of the words, including many in list 4.

TROUBLEMAKERS: 186 Common Words Most Frequently Misspelled by Students*

List 1. Misspelled by 50 to 70 percent of students in grade 8 (15 words)

all right	capital	February	niece	separate
appreciate	chocolate	foreign	pigeon	squirrel
bicycle	exercise	Halloween	scissors	stationery

---

*Harry A. Greene, *The New Iowa Spelling Scale* (Iowa City: Bureau of Educational Research and Service, State Univ. of Iowa, 1954). These percentages were not determined by Greene but have been derived from his data.

List 2. *Misspelled by 40 to 49 percent of students in grade 8 (25 words)*

anxious	carriage	lightning	principal	secretary
auditorium	community	magazine	receive	seesaw
autumn	especially	museum	reindeer	sleigh
balloon	examination	nickel	rooster	umbrella
calendar	handkerchief	post office	scenery	you're

List 3. *Misspelled by 30 to 39 percent of students in grade 8 (38 words)*

against	decide	lawyer	potato	stomach
awful	disease	led	probably	straight
celebrate	English	moss	safety	that's
cellar	fed	naughty	salute	tobacco
chimney	governor	orchestra	Santa Claus	truly
choose	imagine	papa	secret	whose
college	Indian	piece	ski	
course	journey	pleasant	soldier	

List 4. *Misspelled by 20 to 29 percent of students in grade 8 (108 words)*

accident	chose	grocery	overalls	taught
acre	circle	guard	palace	terrible
afraid	citizen	holiday	pardon	theater
allow	colony	hospital	piano	(theatre)
among	costume	hungry	picnic	thirteen
angry	cousin	husband	practice	though
arrive	curtain	kitchen	pumpkin	threw
attention	decorate	knot	quarter	Thursday
August	desert	laid	quiet	toward
automobile	ditch	language	quit	usually
beautiful	divide	leaf	recess	valentine
beauty	easily	lie	Saturday	valuable
believe	either	lit	scarf	violin
Bible	electric	loose	scene	wear
business	engine	lose	scream	Wednesday
cabbage	fifteen	material	she's	we're
canary	finally	merry	since	we've
canoe	foolish	minute	slept	woman
canyon	furniture	multiply	slid	wouldn't
carnival	geography	needle	suppose	wrist
castle	ghost	neighbor	surely	you'd
central	giant	nod	tardy	

Take an inventory.   Which of the 186 troublemakers are in your automatic spelling vocabulary? Find out by taking a test on these words. See if you can get someone to dictate the list to you. If you misspell a word, or if you spell it correctly without being certain that it is correct, star this word on the list on pages 144–145.

Now apply the following four steps to each of the words you misspelled.

1. Pronounce the word by syllables, looking at each syllable as you say it.

2. Write the word from memory, saying each syllable as you write it.

3. Check for correctness.

4. Practice.

Step 1. *Pronounce the word by syllables, looking at each syllable as you say it.*

By doing this, you focus several of your senses at once upon the major parts of the word.

Write the word journey *and underline the syllables.*

Put a double line under any part that is troublesome to you. You may differ from other students in what you consider difficult. The part twice underlined in bureau, technique, enough, *for example, is not pronounced the way it looks. Double-underline the troublesome part in* journey.

As you pronounce the word by syllables, pay special attention to the hard part. Say the word journey *by syllables several times until you have it clearly in mind.*

Step 2. *Write the word from memory, saying each syllable as you write it.*

Now cover the word journey *and write it from memory on the line below.*

Step 3. *Check for correctness.*

Compare your spelling of the word journey *with the dictionary spelling. If there are any errors, or if the word is incomplete, make no correc-*

tions or additions. Instead, put a line through the misspelled word and practice on a scratch pad until you can write the word without a mistake.

Step 4. *Practice.*

One way of practicing is to continue to write from memory and then check. Some students will need to do this only once or twice. Others will not feel certain of a word until they have written it five or ten times without an error. Another means of practice is to write the word in a sentence.

On the lines below, write the word journey *from memory four times and write a sentence using the word.*

1. _____ 3. _____

2. _____ 4. _____

Sentence: _____

_____

_____

Spelling troublemakers. Apply this technique to studying the words that cause you trouble—those whose spelling you are unsure of while writing.

A Bird's-Eye View of Writing a Report

1. Collect and organize information.
2. Make an outline.
3. Organize paragraphs.
4. Make sentences clear.
5. Use words accurately.
6. Supply detail.
7. Rewrite.
8. Learn to spell accurately.

Conclusion: Reevaluating Your Study Habits

You are now ready to evaluate your study procedures again. Test yourself once more with the Study Habits Checklist, beginning on this page.

It is not essential that you place a mark under "Almost Always" opposite each practice in order to prove that you are a good student. As explained in the Introduction, there are individual styles in studying. You must develop your own style. But the checklist does provide you with an opportunity to evaluate, in terms of their helpfulness to you, the study habits that a group of top college students believe to be most important.

Read each question in the checklist. Then answer it by marking an X in the appropriate box.

	Almost Always	More than Half of the Time	About Half of the Time	Less than Half of the Time	Almost Never
Planning Time					
*1. Do you keep up to date in your assignments?					
2. Do you have a study-schedule plan in which you set aside time each day for studying?					

	Almost Always	More than Half of the Time	About Half of the Time	Less than Half of the Time	Almost Never
3. Do you divide your study time among the various subjects to be studied?					

Arranging Physical Setting

4. Is the space on your study desk or table large enough?					
5. Is your study desk or table kept neat, that is, free of distracting objects?					
*6. Do you study in a quiet place — one that is free from noisy disturbances?					
7. Do you study by yourself rather than with others?					
8. When you sit down to study, do you have the equipment and materials you need?					

Previewing

9. Do you read over the table of contents of a book before you begin studying the book?					
10. Before studying an assignment in detail, do you make use of any of the clues in the book such as headings, illustrations, and chapter summaries?					

	Almost Always	More than Half of the Time	About Half of the Time	Less than Half of the Time	Almost Never
Reading					
11. Do you try to get the meaning of important new words?					
12. As you read an assignment, do you have in mind questions that you are actually trying to answer?					
*13. Do you look for the main ideas in what you read?					
14. Are you able to read without saying each word to yourself?					
15. In addition to reading the required textbooks, do you read other materials for your courses?					
Notetaking While Reading					
16. As you read your assignments, do you take notes?					
17. Do you review your notes soon after taking them?					
Remembering					
18. Do you try to find a genuine interest in the subjects you study?					
*19. Do you try to understand thoroughly all material that you should remember?					

	Almost Always	More than Half of the Time	About Half of the Time	Less than Half of the Time	Almost Never
20. When studying material to be remembered, do you try to summarize it to yourself?					
21. Do you distribute the study of a lengthy assignment over several study sessions?					
22. Do you try to relate what you are learning in one subject to what you learn in others?					

Listening and Taking Class Notes

23. During class, do you search for main ideas?					
*24. In class, do you take notes?					
25. Do you revise class notes soon after class?					

Preparing for Examinations

*26. Before an examination, do you review the important facts and principles?					
27. Do you combine important notes on your textbook and from class into a master outline in studying for a major examination?					

	Almost Always	More than Half of the Time	About Half of the Time	Less than Half of the Time	Almost Never
28. Do you make up examination questions that you think will be asked, and answer them?					
29. In studying for an examination, do you distribute your time over at least two sessions?					
Taking Examinations					
*30. In taking examinations, do you read the directions and the questions with care?					
31. At the start of an examination, do you make plans for suitably distributing your time among the questions?					
32. In taking an essay examination, do you outline your answer to a question before you start answering it?					
33. At the end of an examination, do you proof-read or check your answers?					
Report Writing					
34. Before writing a report, do you collect information by doing research in the library?					

	Almost Always	More than Half of the Time	About Half of the Time	Less than Half of the Time	Almost Never
35. Before writing a report, do you make an outline?					
36. In writing a report, do you clearly indicate the main idea of each paragraph?					
37. In writing a report, do you rewrite your first drafts?					

After completing the checklist, compare your responses with those you made when you began this book, pages 3–8. Record below the main changes that have taken place in your study habits.

_____

_____

_____

_____

_____

_____

_____

_____

_____

_____

_____

Practice Materials

CITY PLANNING*

City-Planning Movement

One of the most fruitful means for the improvement of the modern city has been the city-planning movement. Most cities have grown up as chance directed, though a few have benefited by early planning, notably Washington, D.C., Buffalo, Detroit, and Canberra, the capital of Australia.

Although the history of city planning certainly goes back to the cities of the ancient world, the movement did not become an important factor in modern centers of population until the middle of the nineteenth century. Then economic conditions brought about a rapid growth in both European and American cities. Plans were proposed for the future development of Paris in 1853; and a few years later there was much activity in city planning throughout Germany, Italy, and Sweden. In the United States the movement is principally the outgrowth of the genius of Daniel H. Burnham, who designed the remarkably beautiful and noteworthy group of buildings for the World's Columbian Exposition, held at Chicago in 1893.

How Zoning Aids Cities

An important division of the city-planning movement is city zoning. Experts mark out areas that are to be used solely for designated purposes. For examples, stores, homes, schools, police and fire stations, wholesale and warehouse buildings, industrial plants, and produce markets are restricted to certain areas. Zoning also affects the style of architecture. In New York City, for instance, the zoning ordinance establishes a relation between height and ground space that encourages straight (as opposed to set-back) buildings, with large open spaces for promenades and plazas. Since buildings are planned and grouped in relation to their sizes and uses, it is possible to provide for adequate light and fresh air and a display of the beauties of building design. Furthermore, owners of

---

*From *Compton's Encyclopedia*, with permission of F. E. Compton Company, a division of Encyclopaedia Britannica, Inc.

property know for what purposes it may be used, and they can thus plan wisely for its development. Zoning is also an important feature in the safety program of a community.

Public Buildings

Another aspect of city planning is the grouping of public buildings in a civic center. It may include the city hall, courthouse, public library, art museum, churches, high schools, and perhaps university or college buildings. In large cities, municipal government buildings may form one group and other units may be designated for education, art, and community centers.

In the United States there are many outstanding civic centers. Among them are New Orleans' Civic Center, with its city and state government buildings; New York City's Lincoln Center for the Performing Arts, a cultural complex; and Boston's Prudential Center, a community and business center that is a public and private project. A few states plan state capital centers, similar to civic centers.

Transportation and Public Utilities

City planning guides not only civic building activity, but also transportation. This aspect includes the designing and placing of terminals and stations so that the movement of goods and people may be accomplished as efficiently as possible. It also has to do with the location, width, kind, and design of streets; with the planning of public drives and boulevard systems; and with the selection of sites for playgrounds and parks. Special legal measures have been formed whereby under certain conditions a community may condemn property because it constitutes a threat to public health. In such cases compensation is paid to the owners.

Some cities own and operate public utilities, such as gas, water, light and power, and telephone. This is called municipal ownership. Its success depends upon conditions in each locality, the efficiency and intelligence of local government officials, and other factors. Authorities disagree as to the relative merits of municipal versus private ownership of a community's utilities.

Transformation of the City

The city has become the home of art and culture, entertainment, and education. Such advantages have stimulated people to noble endeavor. Many cities have been transformed into communities of great beauty, with opportunities for self-improvement and civic advancement. Thoughtful people try to express through community activities their hopes and aspirations for the more abundant life.

LATITUDE AND LONGITUDE

We can describe any location on the earth as a point at which two lines cross each other. The lines which geographers use to specify locations are *parallels of latitude* and *meridians of longitude.* They are imaginary lines that cross one another. We can use these lines to indicate a point on the earth exactly as we might use streets in locating a corner drug store. If we learn that the store is located at Main and Elm Streets, we will know exactly where to find it.

West-East Lines

A parallel takes the place of one street. Parallels run west and east around the globe. They measure the distance north and south of the equator. The equator is the parallel that lies halfway between the North and South poles. Its number is 0°. In writing the number of a parallel, we put "N" or "S" after it. The letter shows whether the parallel is north of the equator or south of it. Latitude numbers get higher the farther you go north or south of the equator.

In the fifteenth century latitude was still determined by the ancient astrolabe. A navigator could sight the angle of the sun or stars and thereby estimate the latitude. Between then and now, improved instruments and better maps have made it possible for a navigator to determine his latitude with precision.

North-South Lines

Meridians are the lines that cross parallels. The term meridian comes from a Latin word for "midday" or "noon." At midday, when the sun is at the very highest point that it will reach for the day, the shadow cast by a stake driven into the earth will point directly north. The shadow will mark a very short section of a meridian of longitude. (In the southern hemisphere the shadow of any stake points south instead of north at midday.)

As parallels of latitude are numbered from the equator, meridians of longitude are numbered from the prime meridian—the one that passes through Greenwich (a part of London), England. Like the equator, it is numbered zero. Meridians measure distance west and east of the prime meridian. The meridians of longitude divide the circle of the equator into 360°. Most globes show one meridian for every 15°. This is the distance that the earth turns each hour. (Since the earth takes 24 hours to make one complete turn of 360°, it will turn 1/24 of a complete turn in one hour—i.e., $1/24 \times 360° = 15°$.)

Until the sixteenth century, a sailor estimated longitude by guessing the speed of his ship and estimating time by the position of the sun. With improved methods of determining speed, and with the invention of an accurate watch called the chronometer in the eighteenth century, sailors could determine longitude with precision.

Using Latitude and Longitude

Navigators and explorers have always wished to know as precisely as possible where they had been and where particular events of their journeys occurred. At times, their need for this information has been desperate. For example, a ship's crew find themselves lost in the open sea. Their food and water supply is dwindling. The captain is able to figure out their exact position (which means he has determined their latitude and longitude). With the aid of a map and a compass, he heads the ship toward the nearest port.

Sometimes accidents occur. When storm-lashed waves are rolling high, even a steel vessel may be damaged. Also, fires that start aboard ships cannot always be put out. Whenever disaster threatens a vessel, its radio operator broadcasts a call for help. Ships that happen to be near enough are soon speeding to the rescue.

A few years back, on a December day, the Greek cruise ship *Lakonia* took fire and was soon burning fiercely. Other vessels, summoned by the *Lakonia*'s radio, sped to the scene and rescued over 914 survivors. (Over 100 were lost or missing.) Had the radio operator known only that the ship was in the Atlantic Ocean north of the island Madeira, the rescue ships would not have reached the *Lakonia* for days. Because the latitude and longitude were given in the broadcast, the ships knew precisely where to go.

Summary

Parallels of latitude are imaginary lines that run west and east around the earth. The equator is a parallel, numbered 0°. Latitude numbers increase as you go north or south of the equator. The latitude at any point can be determined by measuring the angle of the sun or stars. Meridians are imaginary lines that cross the parallels. They run north and south from pole to pole. The meridian that passes through Greenwich is numbered zero. Distances are measured west and east of longitude 0°. The earth turns 15° longitude every hour – an indispensable bit of knowledge for the navigator in determining longitude. Any point on earth may be indicated by referring to its latitude and longitude. Navigators and explorers are thereby able to identify any point and, in emergencies, to name its exact position in radioing for help.

THE MOON'S MOVEMENTS*

The moon has no fixed place in the sky. It is always moving. Its path, or *orbit*, can be considered only in relation to other heavenly bodies.

The Orbit of the Moon

The moon does not follow a perfect circle in its path around the earth. Its orbit is an *ellipse*, with the earth nearer one end than the other. At the point called the *perigee*, when the moon is nearest the earth, its distance from the earth's center is about 222,000 miles. When it reaches the opposite point, the *apogee*, the moon is about 253,000 miles from the earth's center. The exact distances of the perigee and apogee vary from month to month.

The moon's orbit does not line up with the earth's equator, nor does it align with the earth's path around the sun (the *ecliptic*). It is nearer the latter, however, intersecting the plane of the ecliptic at an angle of about 5°. The two points at which the moon each month crosses the plane of the ecliptic are called the lunar *nodes*.

The moon's path is further complicated. The plane of its orbit wobbles around continuously, as does a spinning coin just before it comes to rest. At a given season, for example, the side of the orbit which lies above (or north of) the ecliptic sometimes points away from the sun and sometimes toward it. This shift occurs slowly, the full cycle of oscillation taking 18.6 years. The cycle is sometimes called the *regression of the nodes*, since the nodes move constantly westward around the ecliptic.

The orbit of the moon at times slants in the same direction as the earth's inclination to the ecliptic. At other times it slants in the opposite direction. As a result, the moon in some years may range farther north and in other years farther south in the sky. The slant and wobble of its orbit also account for the schedule of eclipses. These can take place only when the moon is in line with the sun and earth, or very nearly so.

Eclipses occur at irregular intervals, and they repeat their cycle only approximately every 18 years. The combined number of total or partial eclipses of the sun and the moon cannot exceed seven or be less than two in a calendar year.

Other Variations of the Moon

There are other irregularities in the moon's motion caused by the attraction of the sun and the earth. When the moon is between the sun and the earth, the sun tends to pull it away from the earth. When the

---

*From *Compton's Encyclopedia*, with permission of F. E. Compton Company, a division of Encyclopaedia Britannica, Inc.

moon travels to the far side of the earth, the sun tends to pull it toward the earth. These effects are known as *perturbations.*

The moon shows the same side to the earth at all times. To do this it must rotate once on its axis every time it travels around the earth. If it did not turn, it would show its opposite side every time it traveled halfway around the earth. Actually considerably more than half the moon, or about 59 percent, is seen. This is due to *librations*, or slight tippings back and forth, of the face.

The reason the moon rotates once each time it orbits the earth is unknown. Scientists suspect that the moon's rotation may have adjusted itself to a force such as the earth's gravitational pull. This theory might also explain why the diameter of the moon is bulged an estimated one-third of a mile in the direction of the earth.

The Moon's Timetable

The time it takes the moon to orbit the earth is about $27\frac{1}{3}$ days. This period is called the *sidereal month.* There are about $29\frac{1}{2}$ days, however, between each appearance of the new, or dark, moon, which occurs when the moon appears closest to the sun. This time period is called the *synodic*, or *lunar, month.* It is longer because the earth has also been moving around the sun. Thus the relative positions of the earth, moon, and sun are altered. The moon must travel farther in order to become a new moon.

The daily schedule of the moon also varies. On the average the moon rises about 50 minutes later each night or day. If it were fixed in the heavens like the sun or stars, it would seem to have a more regular schedule.

PSYCHOLOGY*

Psychology is the science that studies why human beings and animals behave as they do. Psychologists are interested in understanding the whole range of human experience, including the reasons for people's motives, thoughts, feelings, and emotions. These problems have puzzled man for centuries. But the scientific study of such problems began only in the mid-1800s.

Psychologists have learned much about behavior and experience, but they have made only a beginning. There is a great deal they know little about, and a lot to be discovered. Suppose you ask yourself: "How does my brain function as a mind?" You would be asking a question that has baffled investigators for hundreds of years. The question is still largely unanswered, but it is being studied by many psychologists collaborating with neurophysiologists and other scientists.

An understanding of why we behave as we do, and why we experience things as we do, has great importance in our daily lives. People want to know how to make better adjustments to situations, and how to learn about themselves so they can reduce their worries and anxieties. They want to discover their skills and aptitudes so they can select a career in which they are likely to be happy and successful. People also want to know how to teach children and how to get along better with each other and achieve lasting peace among nations. Psychologists investigate these problems through careful experimentation and trained observation.

Psychology is sometimes classed with biology, sociology, and anthropology as one of the behavioral sciences. Psychology is also closely related to psychiatry. However, psychiatry is a medical science that deals almost entirely with mental illness. Psychology studies all kinds of human behavior, normal and abnormal. Psychiatrists are physicians with special training in the field of mental illness. Most psychologists have a Ph.D. or M.A. degree, rather than medical-school training.

Methods of Psychology

Psychologists try to establish principles that can be used to explain, predict, and control or change behavior. They follow the general scientific method used by physicists, chemists, and other physical scientists. Psychologists use four main techniques to gather information about behavior: (1) experiments, (2) natural observation, (3) case histories, and (4) surveys.

Experiments. Many interacting conditions and events affect human and animal behavior. To understand behavior, psychologists must discover how these factors influence behavior. The experimental method enables a psychologist to control all the conditions that determine the aspect of behavior he is studying. He can change one condition and observe the effect on another condition while all other factors remain constant.

Natural Observation. Natural observation is the direct observation of human or animal behavior in its natural environment. Psychologists using this method do not attempt to control any conditions of behavior. They must observe and record their observations accurately to avoid basing conclusions on their own prejudices.

Case Histories. When compiling a case history, the psychologist carefully collects information about an individual's past and present life. He or she might observe the person's actions, or interview the individual to gather information about the person's thoughts and feelings. A case history may give a psychologist insight into causes of behavior that cannot be discovered by experiments. For example, the detailed study of a criminal might reveal some causes of various types of behavior.

Surveys. Surveys are often conducted in studies of group behavior or opinions. The psychologist interviews members of a group orally or by written questionnaires. After the data have been analyzed statistically, the pscyhologist can draw conclusions about average attitudes or behavior. He must be careful to select a representative group, so that many shades of opinion can be faithfully gathered.

History

Beginnings. For hundreds of years, people have wondered about the reasons for their thoughts and actions. Until the late 1800s, psychology was an area of study within philosophy.

Plato, Aristotle, and other ancient philosophers developed theories about the causes of behavior and the relationship between mind and body. They believed that the mind was a separate, identifiable thing, located in a specific part of the body.

In the 1600s and 1700s, some philosophers believed the mind was divided into several inborn faculties, including thought, will, and reason, which accounted for different kinds of behavior. During the same period, such philosophers as Thomas Hobbes and John Locke rejected the idea of inborn faculties of the mind. They believed the mind is empty at birth and that a person must have experiences in order to develop ideas. According to these theorists, we get ideas by associating our experiences.

The establishment of psychology as a science based on careful observation and experimentation is generally considered to have taken place in 1879. That year, Wilhelm Wundt, a German philosopher who had studied medicine and physiology, founded what was probably the first psychological laboratory, in Leipzig.

From the late 1800s until the 1930s, four important schools of psychology greatly influenced the development of psychology. These schools were (1) structuralism, (2) behaviorism, (3) gestalt psychology, and (4) psychoanalysis.

Structuralism. Wundt and his students thought psychology's main purpose was to describe and analyze conscious experience — experiences including sensations, images, and feelings of which only the person involved is aware. They regarded conscious experience in the same way as chemists think of such compounds as water. Chemists break water down into hydrogen and oxygen, combined in a certain proportion. Wundt and his students, often called structuralists, tried to do the same for conscious experience. For example, they analyzed the sensation of wetness as the simultaneous experiencing of something cool and the touch of something smooth. This combination of two experiences—temperature and touch—results in the more complex experience of wetness. The primary method of study used by the structuralists was introspection, whereby a person described his or her own experience when stimulated by some object or event.

Behaviorism. Behaviorism was introduced into psychology in 1913 by the American psychologist John B. Watson. It was a reaction against structuralism and the introspective study of conscious experience. Watson called for the study of the observable behavior of humans and animals, not of their experiences.

The behaviorists began laboratory studies of stimulus-response relationships in behavior. Their theories and methods were strongly influenced by the experiments of the Russian physiologist Ivan P. Pavlov. He discovered that animals could be trained to respond to stimuli by association.

Most psychologists agree that their science should study behavior, and rely chiefly on experimental methods. But many think the behaviorists neglected some important questions because they ignored such problems as thought processes and personality development.

Gestalt Psychology. Gestalt psychology was concerned with the organization of mental processes. Like behaviorism, it was also a reaction against structuralism. The German word *gestalt* means pattern or form. Gestalt psychologists believed that human beings and animals tend to perceive organized patterns, not individual parts that are merely added together. According to them, the relationship between different parts of a stimulus, which we perceive as a whole or a pattern, gives us our meanings. The gestaltists attacked the structuralist view that experience could be broken down into its parts, such as seeing, hearing, and feeling. Gestaltists believed that all these factors must be studied together in order to understand their relationships. Max Wertheimer founded gestaltism in Germany about 1912. In the 1930s, Wertheimer and his associates—Wolfgang Köhler, Kurt Koffka, and Kurt Lewin—moved to the United States, where they headed the gestalt movement.

Psychoanalysis. Psychoanalysis began in Europe in the early 1900s under the leadership of Sigmund Freud, an Austrian physician. Freud treated persons who were unable to adjust to the world about them. He developed a theory to explain why people became emotionally disturbed.

According to psychoanalytic theory, a person represses the needs and desires that are unacceptable to himself or society. Freud believed that these unconscious mental processes strongly influence conscious behavior and personality.

Many psychologists today disagree with Freud's theory. But most of them credit him with demonstrating how unconscious events can influence behavior.

Psychology Today

Psychology is a rapidly growing field in which many investigators work on a variety of problems. Some psychologists, influenced by behaviorism, prefer to study observable behavior. They are sometimes called stimulus-response psychologists because they believe all behavior results from stimuli. Other psychologists, sometimes called cognitive theorists, base their ideas on gestalt psychology. They study thought processes such as perceiving, learning, and problem-solving. Many psychologists do not follow any one theory or school of thought. They prefer to establish specific relationships in behavior, rather than broad theories. These psychologists deal with such topics as how we see, how we learn, and how we form attitudes.

Summary

Psychology focuses upon the causes of behavior. Its practitioners experiment systematically to sort out valid causes of behavior from chance causes. Other methods consist of observing a person or animal in its natural environment, gathering case histories from records and interviews, and studying group behavior through interviews and questionnaires.

Not until a hundred years ago did psychology become a science. Four influential schools of thought emerged.

(1) Structuralists, the earliest investigators, sought information from their subjects about their sensations and feelings, and then broke down the data into constituent elements.

(2) The behaviorist school rejected introspection and advocated objective, experimental investigation of stimulus-response relationships through the methods of established science.

(3) Gestalt psychology, also in reaction against structuralism, concluded that the whole of what a person perceives or reacts to is more than the simple combination of its parts – a proposition of great significance to education.

(4) Psychoanalysis demonstrated how unconscious processes can influence behavior.

Much psychological research today is carried out in the behaviorist tradition. Another active group consists of cognitive theorists. Still others seek to uncover specific psychological relationships, remaining outside the framework of any school of thought.

VITAMINS*

All living things, plant or animal, need vitamins for growth, health, and even life. Yet all the vitamins needed by a grown individual each day amount to a mass no larger than a grain of rice.

Vitamins are not food. They do not turn into blood, flesh, and bone or supply energy as foodstuffs do. The body uses them like tools in processes that turn foods into tissues, remove waste products, and produce energy. Vitamins can be used over and over, and only tiny amounts are needed to replace those that break down for some reason.

When a plant or animal does not get all it needs of a certain vitamin, some food-using process starts to run down. In time the running down may become a deficiency disease. This seldom happens, however, to anyone who eats a wide variety of foods. A varied diet supplies all the vitamins a human being needs.

How Foods Supply Vitamins

Vitamins come originally from plants. Plants make all their own foods. They use sunlight, carbon dioxide, water, and minerals in the soil. Therefore they must also make all the vitamins that they require.

Most animals, including human beings, do not have the ability to produce all the vitamins that they need. Animals get their vitamins by eating plants or plant-eating animals.

Scientists did not know that vitamins existed until about the beginning of the twentieth century. They discovered the substances by studying serious diseases such as beriberi, scurvy, and rickets. They found that sufferers from each disease did not eat a certain kind of food. Supplying the particular food cured the particular disease.

Naming Vitamins

Biochemists eventually isolated and learned the chemical make-up of every vitamin discovered. Today they can produce man-made vitamins. It is usually cheaper, however, to get them by extracting the substances from foodstuffs that are rich in them.

When the first vitamins were discovered, scientists simply labeled them with letters of the alphabet. Today some have names that indicate their chemical nature. Others are still called by their letter names because they are shorter and more convenient to use than the chemical terms.

---

*From *Compton's Encyclopedia*, with permission of F. E. Compton Company, a division of Encyclopaedia Britannica, Inc.

The Leading Vitamins

A great many vitamins are known. This article discusses those that are the most important to human beings. The lack of them in the diet is known to cause deficiency diseases.

Vitamin A. Vitamin A aids the eyes. The body uses it in visual purple, a substance that helps the eyes to see in a dim light. Prolonged lack of the vitamin makes the eyes dry, and they are easily infected with disease.

Plants do not produce vitamin A. Leafy green plants, however, do make yellow substances called *carotene* and *cryptoxanthin.* The yellow color is hidden by the green chlorophyll in the leaves. The digestive organs of animals turn these substances into vitamin A.

Vitamin B Complex. So-called vitamin B actually is a mixture of more than ten vitamins. Therefore it is called the vitamin B complex.

Vitamin B_1 (thiamine) helps the body use sugars and starches (carbohydrates) to supply energy. The nervous system particularly depends upon this vitamin. A shortage of vitamin B_1 over a long time may cause beriberi, a deficiency disease of the nerves, especially the nerves of the legs. It occurs chiefly in the Orient, where people live largely on white (polished) rice. This diet lacks B_1 because rice, like other plants, stores vitamins of the B complex in its seed coatings and germ. They are lost when the outer coatings and germ are milled away to make white rice. Milling wheat kernels into white flour has the same result. Today most American-made white flour is enriched with thiamine and other vitamins of the B complex.

Living cells need vitamin B_2 (riboflavin) to help in using oxygen. A serious scarcity may cause soreness of the mouth and tongue and cracked lips, especially at the corners. It may also produce itching and burning of the eyes. These conditions rarely occur because such foods as meat and milk are rich in riboflavin.

Nicotinic acid, or niacin (B_5), prevents or cures pellagra, a deficiency disease that affects people in famine-stricken areas and those too poor to secure a balanced diet. The disease does not occur in people who eat a variety of foods.

Other B complex vitamins include folic acid. Yeast, liver, and many other foods also have it. It prevents and cures anemia in certain animals. Vitamin B_{12} is found in beef liver. It has high value in treating pernicious anemia. The remaining B complex vitamins are required by some animals, but human need for them is uncertain or unknown.

Vitamin C, or Ascorbic Acid. Vitamin C is called ascorbic acid because it is the antiscurvy vitamin (the Latin *scorbutus* means "scurvy"). Scurvy occurs among people who cannot obtain fresh fruits and vegetables. It once was extremely common among sailors on long voyages. Severe scurvy brings softness and bleeding of the gums, hemorrhages from small blood vessels under the skin, and swollen joints. A less severe deficiency may damage the teeth and bones and weaken the blood's resistance to infection. Doctors usually prescribe orange juice, a rich source of vitamin C, for bottle-fed babies because cow's milk contains only about one fourth as much ascorbic acid as mother's milk.

Vitamin D, the "Sunshine Vitamin." Vitamin D is especially important to babies and young children. It regulates the building of calcium and phosphorus into bones and teeth. If the supply is inadequate, the deficiency disease called rickets develops. The bones do not harden properly and are malformed. The teeth, too, may be poor.

The body manufactures vitamin D with the help of sunshine. It takes certain oily substances called sterols, found in both plant and animal foods, and deposits them in the skin cells. Ultraviolet in the sunlight turns the sterols into the vitamin. Ready-made vitamin D exists in some foods, especially egg yolk, certain fishes, and milk products. Vitamin D is often fed to babies and young children to insure growth. The usual source is fish-liver oils. Adults generally get enough vitamin D if they have a moderate amount of sunshine. The body can store it in the summer for use in the winter.

Mini-Lecture: FOREIGN TRADE

Countries must trade with one another for three reasons:

(1) Natural resources are not divided up evenly. Every country has certain natural resources and lacks others.

(2) Climates differ. Hot countries may grow such crops as pineapples and bananas but not wheat. Cool countries may grow such crops as wheat but not tropical fruits.

(3) Countries are at different stages of development. For example, Britain began manufacturing in a big way almost 200 years ago. But many countries in Asia, Africa, and South America haven't yet begun to do so. For these reasons, a country may have too little of some goods and more than enough of others.

Even a land of relative plenty like the United States needs or wants goods from other countries. Our imports include oil, cars, fish, cheese, coffee, and tea. Some of these, you can see, are products that our land can't give us, such as coffee and tea. Other imports are goods that the United States produces but not in large enough amounts. For example, we don't manufacture enough paper, so we buy some from Canada. Some goods we obtain more cheaply by obtaining them from other countries.

Foreign trade also involves exporting goods, of course. Among United States exports are grains, flour, coal, and aircraft.

Most of our exports and imports are carried by ships, called freighters. Some are built for mixed cargo. Others fill their holds entirely with loose coal or grain. Still others, the tankers, carry oil.

Foreign freighters carry on most of the export and import trade. But the United States has a large number of its own ships that, together with its passenger vessels, make up the United States Merchant Marine.

The days of isolation are long since past. No country is required to live on what its own land offers. Day and night, ships sail to and from the shores of the world, carrying goods where they are needed and returning with goods needed elsewhere. Airplanes carry goods that are light or needed to meet an emergency. Trains and trucks handle much of the trade between countries that are not separated by oceans. Foreign trade raises the standard of living of countries throughout the world.

Mini-Lecture: CHANGES IN AGRICULTURE

The population of the United States is growing fast. Yet every census, from 1920 on, has shown fewer farm workers than the census before.

You might suppose that each of us would now have less to eat. But that isn't true. Americans are fed better than ever before. Our farmers can raise more food than we can buy. We sell a great deal to other countries.

What is the answer to this puzzle? In 1820, a farmer walking behind a plow pulled by oxen could feed only about four and one half people besides the farmer. A farmer of today, using tractors, can feed more than twenty-seven people.

Why can one farmer produce so much more today than in earlier times? There are two reasons.

First, there are more farm machines. Machines for planting, cultivation, and harvesting are not new but there are more of them, and they get better and better. The invention of the gasoline engine helped greatly. It could do far more work than the farmer's horse or mule. These animals have almost disappeared from farms today. The tractor has taken their place. One farmer with a tractor can do as much work as several men using animals. Quite a few machines do more than just pull. Look at the giant combines that harvest grain: the corn pickers, and the cotton pickers. Indoor machines are run by electric power. Electricity milks cows, pumps water, grinds feed, and does many other jobs. Nearly all our farms have it.

The second reason why one farmer produces more today than a hundred years ago is that it is now possible to make each acre of farmland produce more. Mr. Jones has a one-man farm. It takes all his time. But suppose he could get more grain or hay or vegetables from every acre. He could then raise more food without much more work.

But can he do this? Yes, he can. By doing better farming, he can raise more on each acre. Scientists have found ways to improve the soil, develop better plants, and fight plant diseases. Inventors have produced better tools for the farm to use. Up-to-date farmers make good use of the discoveries of scientists and inventors. Here are four things that now help American farmers get more from the land.

1. Better seed. Experts have developed much better seed than we used to have. The seed comes from better plants.

2. More water. For thousands of years, farmers have used river water to grow crops in places where there is little or no rainfall. Recently farmers have begun to use irrigation in regions of good rainfall. Even such regions often suffer from long dry spells. Crops then dry up in the fields, and both seed and work are wasted. Now sprinkler pipe is laid across fields. Water is pumped from streams, ponds, or deep wells. The jets of water that shoot from sprinkler pipes save crops in dry weather. They are the reason that we see some fine green fields in the summer even though the country around them is burnt brown by hot sunshine and lack of rain.

3. Better fertilizer. Another way to grow better plants is to give them just the nourishment they should have. Good farmers know what their soil needs to grow healthy plants. They buy the right kinds of fertilizers. Chemical fertilizers are much better than they used to be.

4. Farm chemicals. Growing crops have three enemies — weeds, insects, and disease. Some weeds hurt food crops by shading them. They grow faster than the crops and cut off the sunlight. Others strangle crops by clinging to their stalks. All weeds take nourishment that should go to the useful plants. In the old days, weeds were fought with the hoe. Machines called cultivators now help farmers do the job faster. Chemicals kill weeds with even less work.

It costs American farmers several billion dollars a year to feed insects that they don't want. Some insects chew up plants. Others suck the juices from them. Still others, like the apple worm, spoil fruit by boring into it. These enemies can be killed in huge numbers by spraying liquid chemicals or spreading powder over crops.

Sickness is much more deadly among plants than among human beings. We usually get well, but sick plants are likely to die. Seeds are often treated with chemicals to protect the plants from disease. Chemicals are sprayed on growing crops, too.

Useful as farm chemicals are, they often cause trouble. Poisons that kill insects may harm birds that eat the insects. When poisonous chemicals are washed by rain into rivers, they are often harmful to fish. People, too, are in danger from overuse of pesticides. Scientists are now at work to find how and what chemicals can be safely used, and are seeking substitutes for harmful pesticides.

QUIZ ON "PSYCHOLOGY"

Maximum score: 100 points.

A maximum of 80 points will be given for part A.
One point will be given for each correct item in part B.
Time limit: 45 minutes.

Part A

1. Contrast the methods of investigation and the beliefs of structuralists, behaviorists, gestaltists, and psychoanalysts. (60 points)
2. Give an example of how psychological research has contributed (or could contribute) to the solution of a practical human problem. (20 points)

Part B

Write the letter of the correct answer before each item.

_____ 1. Psychology is a branch of (a) psychiatry, (b) anthropology, (c) the behavioral sciences, (d) philosophy.

_____ 2. The scientific study of psychology may be said to have begun in (a) ancient times, (b) 18th century, (c) 19th century, (d) 20th century.

_____ 3. Gestalt psychology emphasizes (a) introspection, (b) stimulus-response relationships, (c) perception of organized patterns, (d) unconscious motivation.

Complete the following sentences.

The techniques of research used by psychiatrists are 4. _____

5. _____

6. _____

7. _____

8. Psychiatry, unlike psychology, deals almost entirely with problems of

_____

Indicate whether each of the following statements is true or false by marking T or F on the line before it.

_____ 9. Psychological research requires that subjects be interviewed.

_____ 10. Plato was the first psychologist.

_____ 11. Locke believed that the mind is empty at birth.

_____ 12. Behaviorism was introduced in the nineteenth century.

_____ 13. Wundt was a leading structuralist.

_____ 14. Behaviorists emphasize stimulus-response relationships.

_____ 15. Cognitive theorists study thought processes.

Match the items in the left-hand column with those in the right-hand column by placing the appropriate letter before each name.

_____ 16. Freud

(a) Ideas are obtained by associating experiences.

_____ 17. Hobbes

(b) We learn about sensations, etc., by analyzing conscious experience into its parts.

_____ 18. Watson

(c) Psychology should concentrate on the scientific study of behavior.

_____ 19. Wertheimer

(d) A mental process is more than the sum of its parts.

_____20. Wundt

(e) The mind consists of a number of inborn faculties.

(f) Unconscious events influence behavior.

After you complete the quiz, return to the article on "Psychology" on page 159, correct your quiz, and compute your score.

QUIZ ON "VITAMINS"

Time: 45 minutes. Maximum score: 50 points.

Part I

Maximum score: 20 points (1 point for each correct item).

Indicate whether each of the following is true or false, by marking before it + (for true) or 0 (for false).

_____1. The human body is equipped to produce all the vitamins it needs.

_____2. Vitamins can be made in chemical laboratories.

_____3. The human body requires a large daily mass of vitamins.

Check the correct answers to the following two questions.

4. What body organ is particularly dependent on vitamin A?

_____ liver

_____ eyes

_____ kidneys

_____ heart

5. What is a common sympton of vitamin C deficiency?

_____ scurvy

_____ rickets

_____ obesity

_____ beriberi

Complete the following sentences.

6. Important in the prevention or treatment of pernicious anemia is

   vitamin _____ , known also as _____ _____ . It

   occurs in many foods, including _____ .

Match the items in the left-hand column with those in the right-hand
column.

_____ 7. In orange juice and cod-liver oil   (a) Vitamin A

_____ 8. Prevents pellagra   (b) Vitamin B$_1$

_____ 9. Manufactured by the body   (c) Vitamin B$_2$

_____ 10. Assists body's use of carbohydrates   (d) Vitamin C

                                                  (e) Vitamin D

                                                  (f) Niacin

Part II

A maximum of 20 points will be given for each of the two items.

1. Describe the body's manufacture of the "sunshine vitamin," tell
   where it is found ready-made, and explain its role in health.

2. Describe the symptoms of vitamin B$_1$ deficiency, and explain how
   it may be prevented through diet.

After completing the quiz, return to the article on "Vitamins" on page
164, correct your quiz, and compute your score.

2608